MW01156669

Henry Mancini

SOUNDS AND SCORES

A practical guide to
professional orchestration

All music composed and
arranged by the author

NORTHRIDGE MUSIC, INC.

to ginny

GUIDE TO THE RECORDED EXAMPLES
CD TRACK INDEX

HENRY MANCINI

BIOGRAPHY

By any set of standards, Henry Mancini is regarded by his peers and music critics as one of the giants of the popular music field.

For his film work, he has been honored by the Academy of Motion Picture Arts and Sciences with 16 Academy Award nominations and 4 of the coveted golden Oscars. Mr. Mancini has produced seven gold albums and has won 20 Grammys, the Hollywood Foreign Press Association's Golden Globe, and practically every other honor the entertainment industry can bestow.

Mancini is also a familiar television personality. He has hosted his own half-hour TV music series, "Mancini Generation," plus several hour-long specials. He has conducted the Academy Awards music program many times. He also makes numerous appearances on the popular interview and talk shows, as well as on many network and syndicated variety specials and series.

His concerts are SRO in cities coast to coast and around the world, whether he is conducting at the Hollywood Bowl, on a leading university campus, at the John F. Kennedy Center for the Performing Arts, or in the capitals of any of a dozen foreign countries. Among the symphony orchestras he has conducted are The Philadelphia Orchestra, The Boston Pops, The Cleveland Orchestra, The Pittsburgh Symphony, The Los Angeles Philharmonic Orchestra, The Israel Philharmonic, The London Symphony Orchestra, and The Royal Philharmonic Orchestra of London. In 1966, 1982 and 1984 he appeared for Royal Family Command Performances at the London Palladium.

His deep love of music and his concern for budding musicians is perhaps best shown through his book, *Sounds and Scores - A Practical Guide to Professional Orchestration* (published by Northridge Music, Inc.), which can be found on the shelves of virtually every serious student of music and professional performer. Mancini scholarships and fellowships are benefiting many of tomorrow's composers, conductors and arrangers studying at New York's famous The Juilliard School, the West Coast's UCLA and USC, and the American Federation of Music's "Congress of Strings."

Henry Mancini was born in Cleveland, Ohio on April 16, 1924. His father, Quinto, and his mother, Anna, soon moved to the steel town of Aliquippa, PA. At the age of eight, Henry was first introduced to music and the flute by his father, who played the instrument himself.

When he was 12, Mancini took up piano and within a few years became interested in arranging. A need for instruction and guidance led the developing musician to Max Adkins, who was conductor and arranger for the house orchestra at the Stanley Theatre in Pittsburgh.

Soon after graduation from Aliquippa High School in the fall of 1942, Mancini enrolled in The Juilliard School of Music. His studies were interrupted by a service draft call in 1943. He served overseas in the Air Force and later in the Infantry. Following his release from the Armed Forces in 1945, Mancini joined the Glenn Miller-Tex Beneke Orchestra as a pianist-arranger. Ginny O'Connor, who was singing with the band and was one of the original members of Mel Torme's "Mel Tones" singing group, soon became his wife.

They were married in Hollywood in 1947 and now live in Holmby Hills, Calif. They have three children: a son, Chris and twin daughters, Monica and Felice.

Mancini's private studies continued with composers Ernst Krenek, Mario Castelnuovo-Tedesco and Dr. Alfred Sendry. In 1952 Mancini joined the music department of Universal-International Studios. During the next six years he contributed to over 100 films, most notably *The Glenn Miller Story* (for which he received his first Academy Award nomination), *The Benny Goodman Story* and Orson Welles' *Touch of Evil.*

Soon after leaving Universal-International, Mancini scored the TV series, "Peter Gunn" for producer-director Blake Edwards, a relationship which was to culminate in later years with the "Pink Panther" features. His use of the jazz idiom for the "Gunn" TV series created an instant success and resulted in a nomination for an Emmy Award from the Academy of Television Arts and Sciences.

The album "The Music from Peter Gunn" was released in 1958 by RCA Victor and earned him a gold record. The album was voted two Grammys by the members of the National Academy of Recording Arts and Sciences as Album of the Year and Best Arrangement of the Year.

The success of "Peter Gunn" was repeated in 1960 by another Edwards-Mancini collaboration, "Mr. Lucky." The album "Music from Mr. Lucky" joined "Peter Gunn" as a best seller. The National Academy of Recording Arts and Sciences again honored Mancini with two Grammys for Best Arrangement and Best Performance by an Orchestra. His album "The Blues and the Beat" was also awarded a Grammy that same year.

Billboard paid tribute to the "Mr. Lucky" album by naming it Instrumental Album of the Year. In addition, the 1964, 1965, 1967, 1968, 1969 and 1970 *Playboy* Readers' Jazz Poll voted Mancini leader of the All-Star Orchestra.

The composer-arranger's return to motion picture scoring has so far produced the following movie scores: *High Time, The Great Impostor, Mr. Hobbs Takes A Vacation, Bachelor in Paradise, Breakfast at Tiffany's, Experiment in Terror, Days of Wine and Roses, Charade, The Pink Panther, Soldier in the Rain, Dear Heart,*

Shot in the Dark, Moment to Moment, The Great Race, Arabesque, What Did You Do in the War, Daddy?, Two for the Road, Wait Until Dark, Gunn, The Party, Me, Natalie, Gaily, Gaily, The Molly Maguires, Sunflower, Darling Lili, The Hawaiians, The Night Visitor, Sometimes a Great Notion, The Thief Who Came to Dinner, Oklahoma Crude, and *Visions of Eight,* the official feature film of the 1978 Olympics. More recent scores include *The White Dawn, The Great Waldo Pepper, The Return of the Pink Panther, Once Is Not Enough, The Pink Panther Strikes Again, Silver Streak, House Calls, The Revenge of the Pink Panther, Who Is Killing the Great Chefs of Europe?, Nightwing, Prisoner of Zenda, 10, S.O.B., Victor, Victoria, Lifeforce, Santa Claus—The Movie,* and *A Fine Mess.*

In 1962 The Academy of Motion Pictures Arts and Sciences recognized Mancini's ability by awarding him two Oscars — one for Best Original Score, *Breakfast at Tiffany's,* and another for Best Song, "Moon River" (lyrics by Johnny Mercer). He was also nominated by the Academy for the song "Bachelor in Paradise" (lyrics by Mack David).

The National Academy of Recording Arts and Sciences followed up the golden statuette honors by awarding Mancini five Grammys for his recorded versions of the same movie and score. "Moon River" was named Record of the Year, Song of the Year and Best Arrangement. "Breakfast at Tiffany's" was awarded Best Performance by an Orchestra for Other Than Dancing and Best Soundtrack LP of a Score from a Picture or TV.

In 1962, the Academy again awarded Mancini an Oscar for Best Song for "Days of Wine and Roses" (lyrics by Johnny Mercer.)

The Academy awarded yet another Oscar to Mancini in 1983 for Best Original Song Score for "Victor, Victoria." (lyrics by Leslie Bricusse).

To date, Mancini has received 20 Grammys. His gold records now total seven: "The Music from Peter Gunn," "Breakfast at Tiffany's," "The Pink Panther," "The Best of Mancini," "Love Theme from Romeo and Juliet," "A Warm Shade of Ivory," "A Merry Mancini Christmas."

In 1984 Henry Mancini achieved the #1 position on the classical music charts with "Mamma," which he recorded with Luciano Pavarotti. This album has achieved gold status in Italy.

Henry Mancini is unusual in that he is one of the few members of the entertainment community who, after his resounding success in motion pictures, has never turned his back on his TV beginnings. He continues to be very active in television, writing the theme music for many of the popular series as well as specials and long-form films. These have included such disparate ventures as "Hotel," "Newhart," "Remington Steele," "Ripley's Believe It or Not," "Cade's County,"

"Curiosity Shop," "NBC Mystery Movie," "What's Happening," "Sanford Arms," "The Moneychangers," "A Family Upside Down," "The Best Place To Be," "The Blue Knight," the critically-acclaimed "The Thorn Birds," and even the "NBC News Election Coverage Theme."

To add to his honors, Mancini has also received four honorary doctoral degrees: an Honorary Doctor of Music from Duquesne University in Pennsylvania in 1976, an Honorary Doctor of Humane Letters from Mount Saint Mary's College in Maryland (1980), an Honorary Doctor of Humanities from Washington and Jefferson College in Pennsylvania in 1981, and, in 1983, an Honorary Doctorate from California Institute for the Arts in Valencia.

In 1985 Mancini was appointed the Grand Marshall of New York City's Columbus Day parade, and was the recipient of The Leadership Award from the Columbus Citizens Foundation, sponsor of the 40-year-old Fifth Avenue parade.

Henry Mancini's leisure time is occupied by photography, skiing and painting. His wine cellar is among the best in Southern California.

He is also an avid art collector. His collection includes four pieces of sculpture by Rodin, and oils by Dauchot, Caffe, Barnabe, Dubuffet, Foujita, Spencer, Marchand, Potast, Gen-Paul and his two personal favorites — a small still life by James Cagney and a water color by Johnny Mercer.

FOREWORD

Following the score along with the recording of a piece of music has long been a major part of the "serious" music student's method of study. Unfortunately, the young "popular" music student who hopes to become a professional composer-arranger in the commercial field has no wealth of material to aid him. Printed scores of commercial recordings are rare. The basic purpose of this book is to remedy this situation by giving the budding professional a means of comparing the recorded sounds with the printed illustrations. However, this procedure will be altered from time to time to include discussion of subjects that are not available on recordings.

Since the average dance orchestra does not include eight brass, five saxes, four French horns, or twenty strings, many of the recorded examples are rewritten for smaller groups, showing how the voicings change as the groups get progressively smaller.

We will not concern ourselves with definitive studies of the technical possibilities of the various instruments. The orchestration books of Cecil Forsyth and Walter Piston have taken ample care of this for us. Our main concern is the combining of the instruments into sections and ensembles of all the types that must be dealt with by the professional writer in the commercial field.

Practically all of the examples are in concert *-sketch form. This method clearly illustrates at a glance exactly what is being played and by whom. No transposition is necessary except in the cases of those instruments that normally sound an octave higher or lower than written.

Our examples are taken from these RCA Victor albums:

The Music from Peter Gunn	No. 1956
More Music from Peter Gunn	No. 2040
The Music from Mr. Lucky	No. 2198
The Blues and the Beat	No. 2147
The Mancini Touch	No. 2101

A deep and grateful bow must be made in the direction of the musicians who performed on these records. They are not capable of less than perfection.

No matter how many books a person has read on this subject and no matter how many recordings he has heard and analyzed, his progress can only be measured by what he writes and has performed. If this book can take a few of the stumbling blocks out of his path and light the way a bit, my purpose will have been fulfilled.

Manuscript pages have been inserted in various places to permit the reader to make any notations he may wish

*The term "concert" means that all of the instruments are written in the same key as the piano.

Additional cassette tapes are available through your music dealer

TABLE OF CONTENTS

The Essentials

CHAPTER ONE
The Essentials

ASIDE FROM HIS OWN ORIGINAL INSTRUMENTALS THE ARranger usually works from a printed piano-vocal leadsheet. If the song is unfamiliar, play it over several times until your ear can follow the melody and the harmonic progressions easily. Check the chord symbols above the vocal line carefully. For some reason these chords do not always match the written-out chords below them. If you find a discrepancy, let your ear be the judge as to what is correct.

This is also true of the bass line. If it doesn't seem to be the best possible bass note for the progression, play around until you find one that is.

If your singer is doing a song in a key other than the one that is printed, write the entire tune out in the new key with the chord symbols above and get familiar with it. Do this before you start the arrangement and you will save much time.

There are three methods of scoring:

1. Sketch in concert on four- or five-staff sketch paper (in much the the same way that our recorded examples are set up) and then transfer to the actual score paper, in concert or transposed key.
2. Score directly in concert.
3. Score directly transposed.

The first method takes the most time, since you actually write out the arrangement twice. This method is used almost exclusively in motion pictures because time does not usually permit one man both to compose and to orchestrate an entire score. The composer sketches in concert and then turns it over to his orchestrator for scoring.

Scoring directly in concert is a bit uncommon. The main reason is that a concert score must be transposed by the copyist, thereby raising the copying costs by about one half.

By far the fastest, most efficient, and most widely used method is the transposed score. Get into the habit of scoring this way from the very beginning.

When approaching an instrumental, do a little ground work before you start filling in. Lightly pencil in your leads and spot your solos on the score paper from beginning to end if possible. This simplified sketching gives you a general conception of the over-all form of your score.

There are several helpful short-cuts that are in general use. When a section is playing in unison it is not necessary to write out the same part for each of the instruments in that section.

Using the *Peter Gunn* theme as our example, here are two ways of doing this:

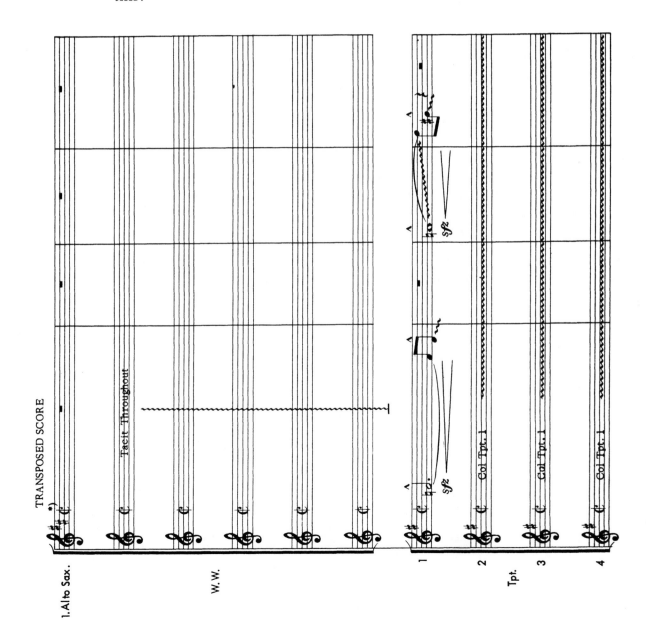

EXAMPLE 1 *PETER GUNN*

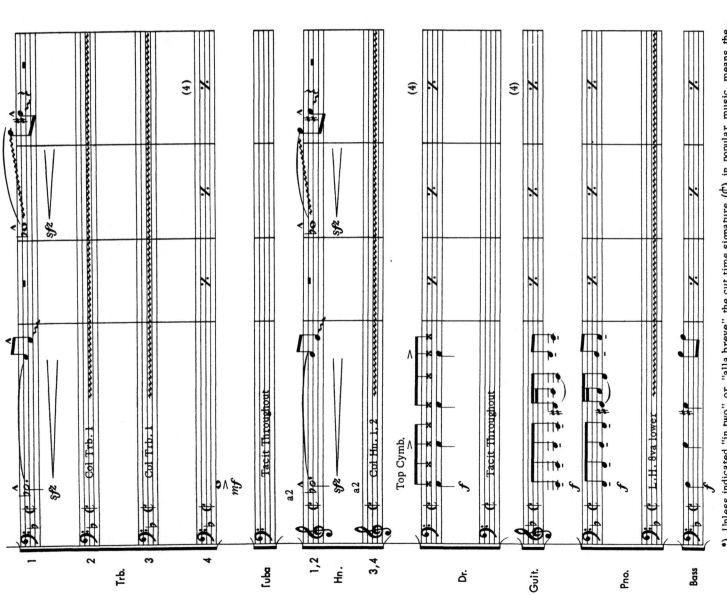

*) Unless indicated "in two" or "alla breve", the cut time signature (¢) in popular music means the same as ⁴⁄₄ or C. The ¢ is usually used for the faster tempos, the ⁴⁄₄ or C for slower tempos (ballads).

EXAMPLE 2   *PETER GUNN*

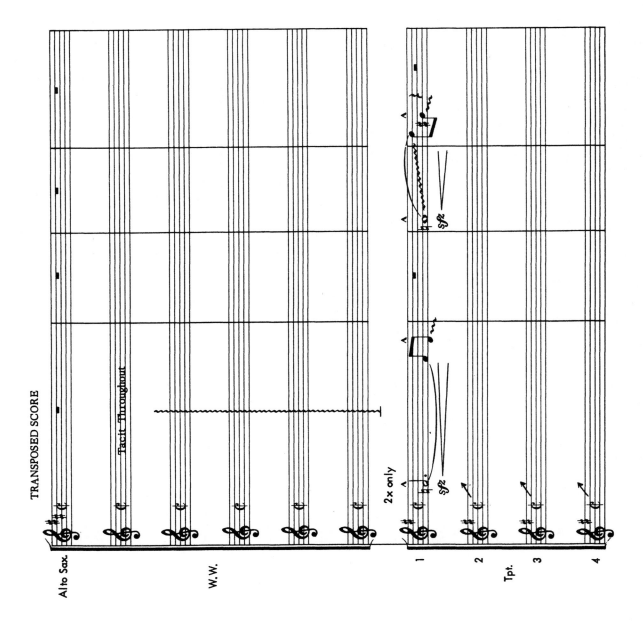

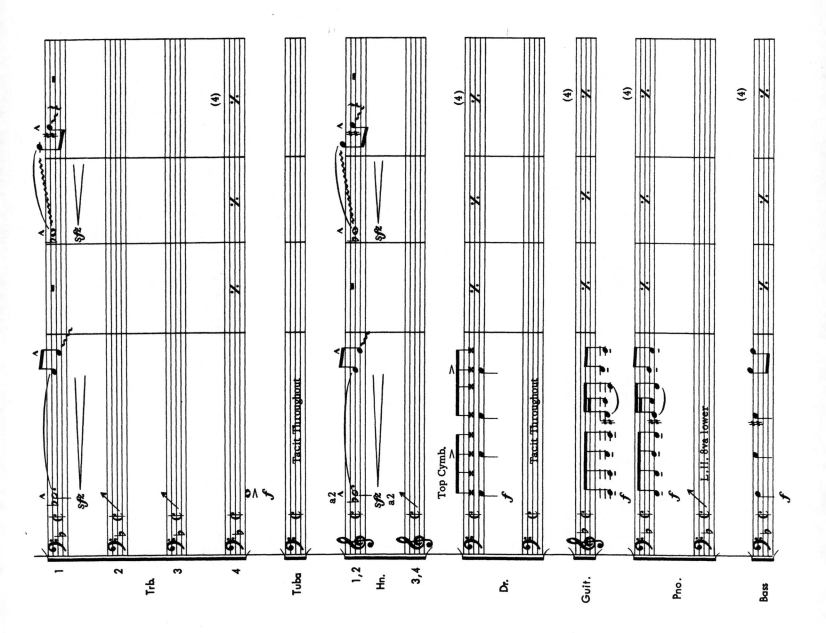

There are two ways of marking scores and parts for rehearsal and cutting purposes. Letters may be used every eight bars or the bars may be numbered. The numbered-bar system is used by most professionals because it permits the instant pinpointing of any bar or note in the score.

The *come sopra* ("as before") is used when repeating bars that have been previously used in the score. They are notated in the following ways:

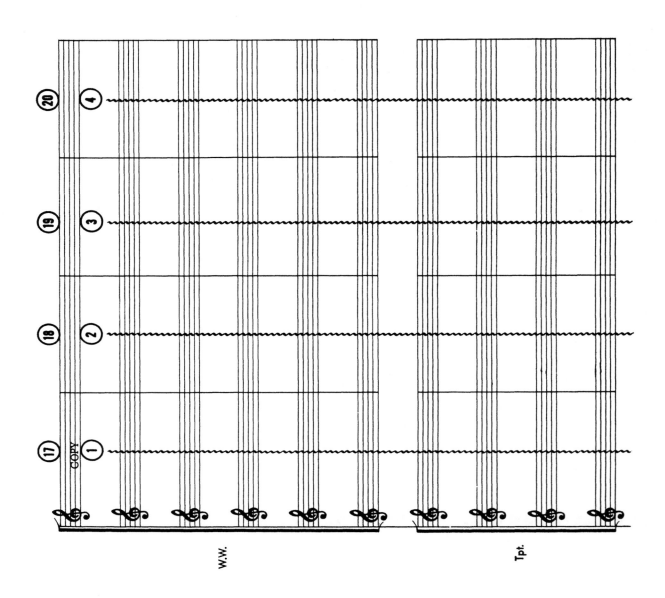

EXAMPLE 3   *PETER GUNN*

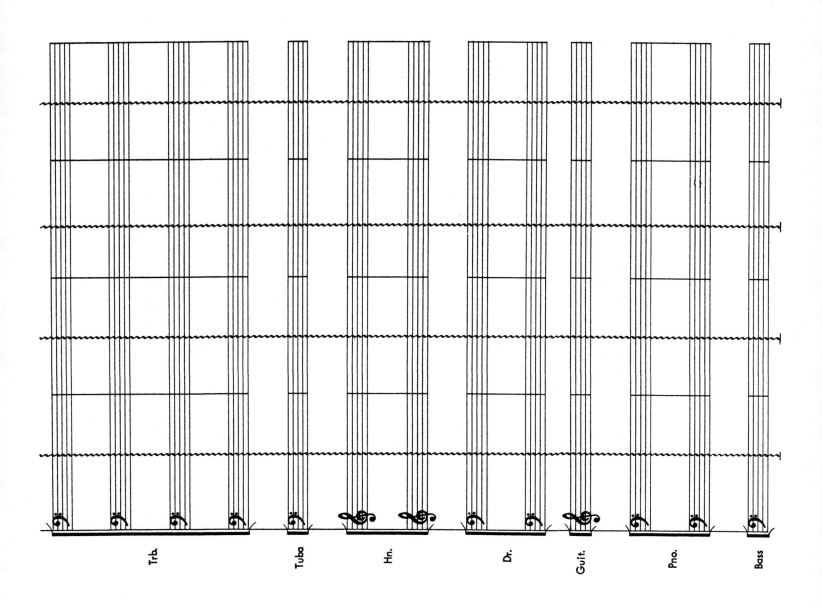

EXAMPLE 4 *PETER GUNN*

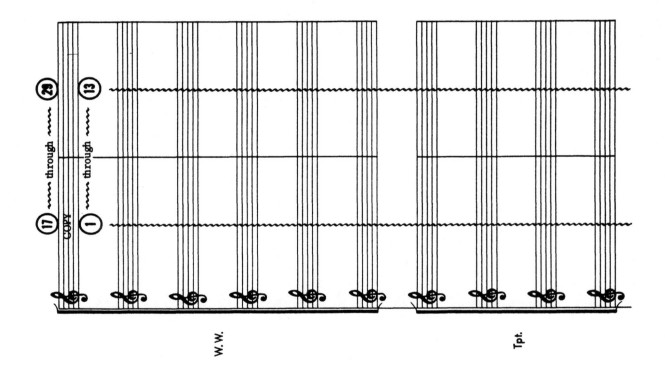

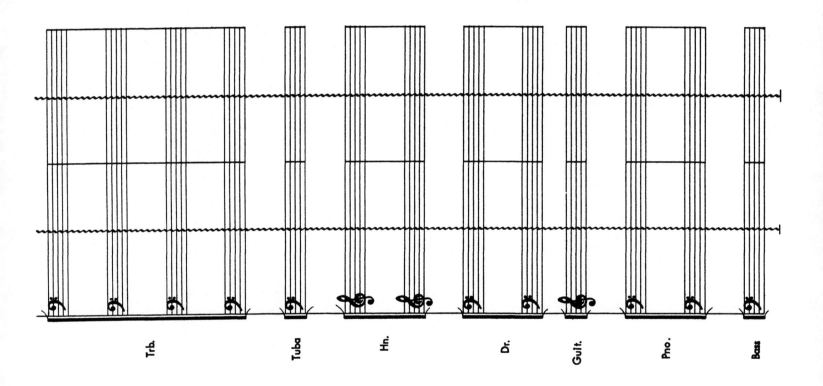

Trb.   Tuba   Hn.   Dr.   Guit.   Pno.   Bass

In the interest of clean and precise playing, get into the habit of notating the exact value of notes, especially on endings.

Without a conductor there will be many conceptions within the band about where this note should end:

EXAMPLE 5

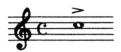

If you want it to end on the downbeat, write:

EXAMPLE 6

On the fourth beat:

EXAMPLE 7

There is no doubt about where either of these notes is cut off. The same rule applies to notes of lesser duration.

Mark phrasing, dynamics, and accents carefully. If a substitute player is called in and is faced with a poorly marked part, the results will be sad indeed.

There are two methods of indicating ad lib solos.

EXAMPLE 8

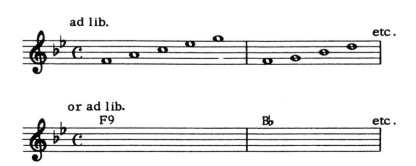

From time to time you will encounter a soloist who plays a transposing instrument who prefers the chords in concert key rather than the transposed key of his instrument. Write it the way your man prefers.

One thing that cannot be stressed too strongly is the final checking of the score before it goes to the copyist. A few wrong notes can be expected, even from professionals, but a barrage of wrong notes can cause a big waste of time and may even result in the discarding of an otherwise good score.

A sensible rehearsal procedure must be followed in order to get the full potential out of an arrangement. Take it easy. Don't bury your head in the score the first time through. Listen carefully and by all means try to get all the way through the number before you start the cleaning-up process. Many of the rough spots will disappear on the second reading. Don't close your mind to the suggestions of your musicians. Hear them out and then decide whether or not their ideas are good ones.

Finally, don't fall in love with every note you write. The professional writer must be a first-class editor. Be prepared to eliminate anything that tends to clutter up your score, painful as it may be to do so.

The Saxophones

CHAPTER TWO
The Saxophones

BE IT AN ALTO, TENOR, OR BARITONE, THE SAXOPHONE HAS A wide dynamic range. From the almost whispering sub-tone to the full-bodied wail, it offers the writer a greater degree of shading than perhaps any other wind instrument in the band.

The ranges and transposition of the saxophone family:

EXAMPLE 9   *THE SAXOPHONES*

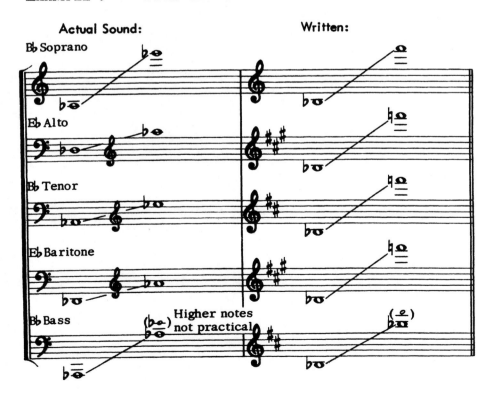

An obvious and most effective device for saxophones is the octave unison. A typical example of unison saxes carrying the lead is found in "Spook" (*More Music From Peter Gunn*).* A sinister sound is provided by the one alto and one tenor sax on the top octave and two baritone saxes on the lower octave.

EXAMPLE 10   *SPOOK!*   Side A, Band 1

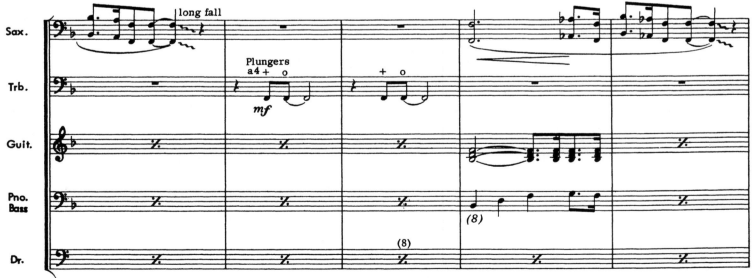

* If an example is taken from a recording, the title of the album from which it was taken will follow the title of the number.

Although two baritone saxes were used on the lower octave, practically the same effect can be had with one. This is a strong register for the baritone. He can hold his own even with four saxes on the upper octave. One point, however: although the baritone does go down to the concert Db below the low F in this piece, you had better know your player well before writing below the F. Only the better players can move around down there with ease. Only the best can play softly in that register. This also applies to some extent to the lower end of the alto and tenor saxes although they are usually more at ease.

When using the extremes, either high or low, on any instrument, the writer must know his player's ability. If you are writing for a band with which you are not familiar, play it safe! A score is judged on how well it sounds, not on how hard it is to play.

A good example of the perfect unison (everyone on the same note) will be found behind Pete Candoli's exciting trumpet solo in "Blue Steel" (*More Peter Gunn*).

EXAMPLE 11   *BLUE STEEL*   Side A, Band 1

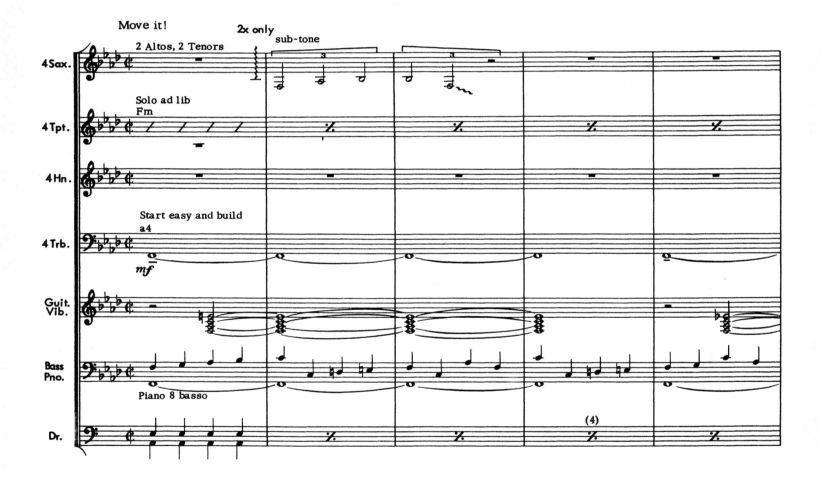

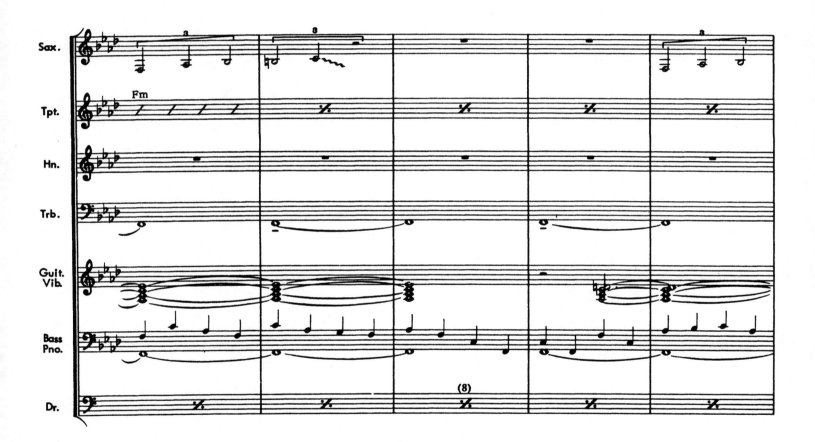

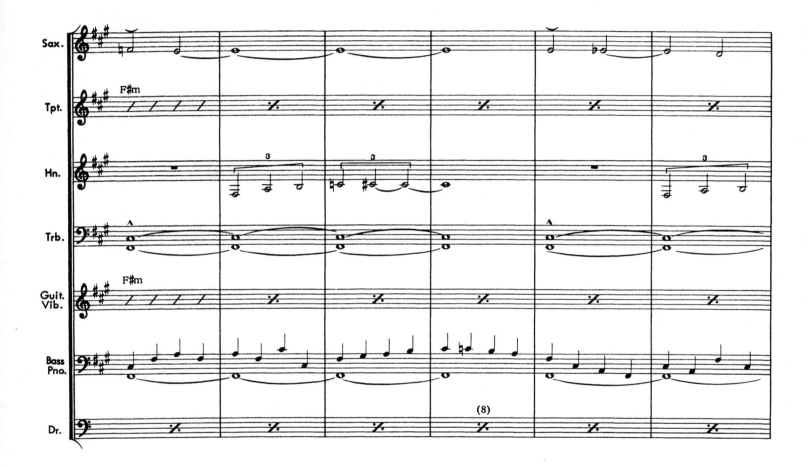

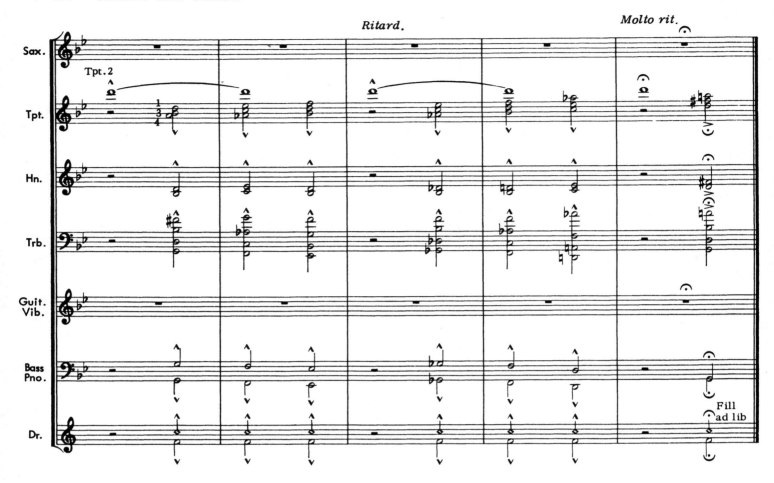

For an occasional change of color, especially in ballads, the saxes can be voiced in thirds. Two or three altos on top and two or three tenors a third below make a very pleasant sound.

EXAMPLE 12

---

*The mark ⌣ indicates that the note is to be sounded a bit under pitch and then lipped up to its true pitch. This is called *bending* a note.

The same passage would be ideal played in octaves with two clarinets on the top thirds and two tenors on the bottom. This is a pretty sound with a good bit of brilliance. (The octave unison between the clarinets and tenors has the same quality with a lot more brilliance in the high register.)

EXAMPLE 13

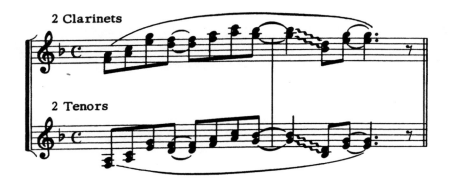

The wonderful thing about the saxes when it comes to four- or five-part section writing is that they blend well with each other in practically any combination. (Alto-Alto-Tenor-Tenor; A A T B; A T T B; T T T B; A A T T B; A A T T T; A T T T B; T T B B; etc.)

This brings up the question of how we "voice" (distribute) a given chord.

The closest of all voicings is the cluster:

EXAMPLE 14

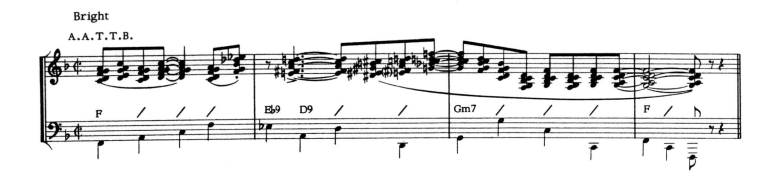

The most basic voicing, not only for saxes but for all sections, is the five-part close (block) type. "Blues for Mother's" illustrates this:

EXAMPLE 15   *BLUES FOR MOTHER'S*

This type of voicing, when applied to an up-tempo number, becomes buoyant and swinging. The Benny Goodman and Artie Shaw bands made wonderful use of it, most of the time with only four saxes (A A T T). The double lead on the bottom in a five-man section, while giving body to the section, is not indispensable.

By putting a clarinet on the lead and using two altos and two tenors below we have the clarinet lead voicing used so beautifully by Glenn Miller.

In the previous example a problem is created by the key of the piece. The baritone is near the top of his range and does not sound good up there. Rather than change to a lower key and lose the brilliance of the high alto sax lead, we take the first harmony note under the lead alto, drop it an octave and give it to the baritone:

EXAMPLE 16   *BLUES FOR MOTHER'S*

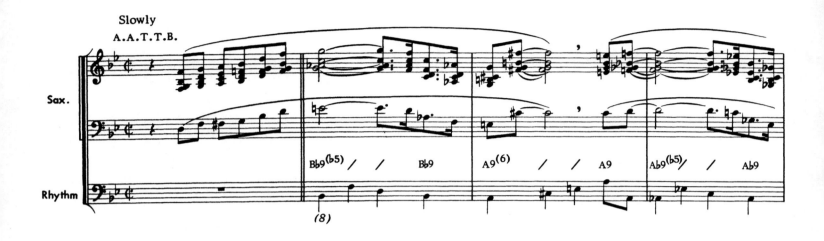

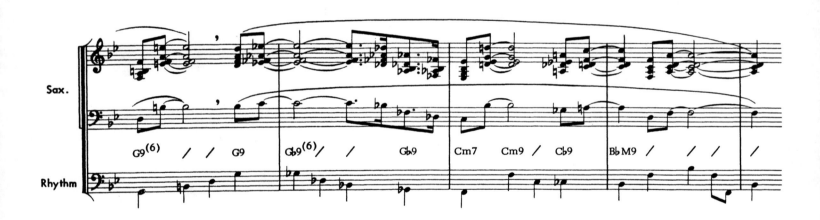

This takes a bit away from the over-all brilliance of the sound, but in its place we now have a little deeper and more mellow one.

If you have only four saxes to work with, you can open them in this way:

EXAMPLE 17   *BLUES FOR MOTHER'S*

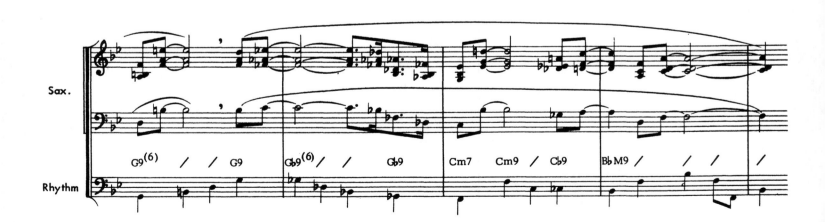

Getting back to our five-man section, let's open it up a bit more:

EXAMPLE 18   *BLUES FOR MOTHER'S*

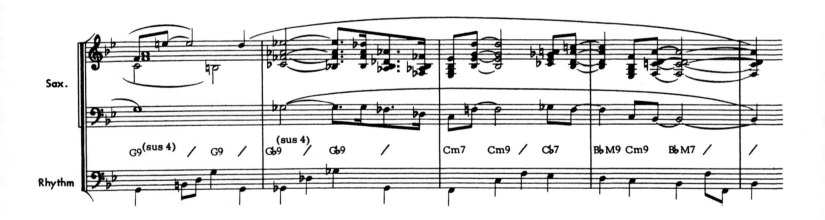

As you can see by the fourth part, we now have some room to add a passing tone. Another point of interest here is the way the lead alto passes through some of the other voices. The balance of the chord is not disturbed by the wandering alto, because the four lower voices are forming the background for the lead alto solo.

Next, with some harmonic variations, is the widest of the open voicings. This is a wonderfully deep sound that is extremely useful:

EXAMPLE 19   *BLUES FOR MOTHER'S*

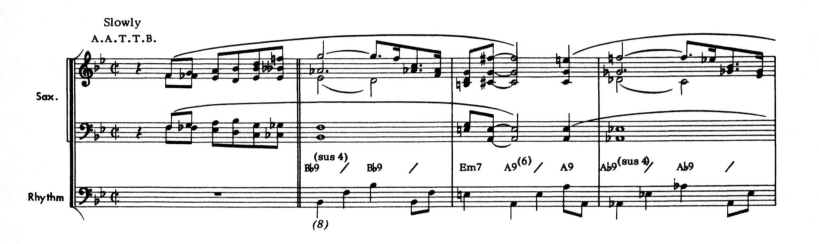

Here are several different types of voicings combined behind a soloist or vocalist. Notice the movement of the counter line when the melody line is stationary:

EXAMPLE 20   *BLUES FOR MOTHER'S*

These are the most basic voicings. They will also work for your brass, woodwind, or string sections having the same number of parts. Which one to use is something the writer must decide for himself. The real skill comes in combining the various types of voicings into a sensible, playable arrangement. One last point in general: it has been my experience that while the open voicings are fine for pretty numbers, they tend to slow things down when applied to the faster tempos.

The Woodwinds

CHAPTER THREE

The Woodwinds

THERE WAS A TIME NOT LONG AGO WHEN A SAXOPHONIST was only required to play his own sax and maybe double on clarinet. Times have changed. The woodwind section of the *Peter Gunn* orchestra points up just how far this business of doubling has come. Our four players, Ted Nash, Ronnie Lang, Harry Klee, and Gene Cipriano, play a total of twenty-seven instruments. As well as the various saxes, each plays piccolo, C flute, alto flute, and bass flute. We have two bass clarinets and finally an oboe and an English horn. Needless to say, this is quite an unusual group of artists.

My point is that the woodwind player now offers a writer a wide variety of tonal colors.

The Flutes

The flute family has made great strides in popularity in recent years. In the hands of our jazz artists the flute has been fully accepted as a solo instrument in that idiom.

The Piccolo

The baby of the family, the piccolo, has long been known as the maverick voice playing high above the rest of the military band. The piccolo range and transposition:

EXAMPLE 21   *THE PICCOLO*

There is also a piccolo built in D♭. The range is the same but a transposition of one-half tone down is necessary.

The piccolo has an extremely piercing quality, especially in the top half of its range. When two, three, or four piccolos are combined in perfect unison they produce a gay, whistling sound.

Good evidence of this can be found in the opening melodic statement of "Timothy" (*More Peter Gunn*). Later on in the release of the same piece they go into thirds, giving us an entirely new color.

EXAMPLE 22   *TIMOTHY*   Side A, Band 2

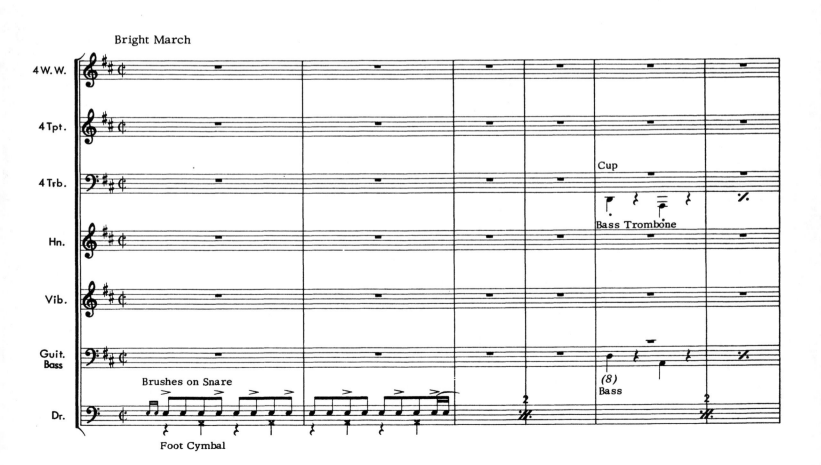

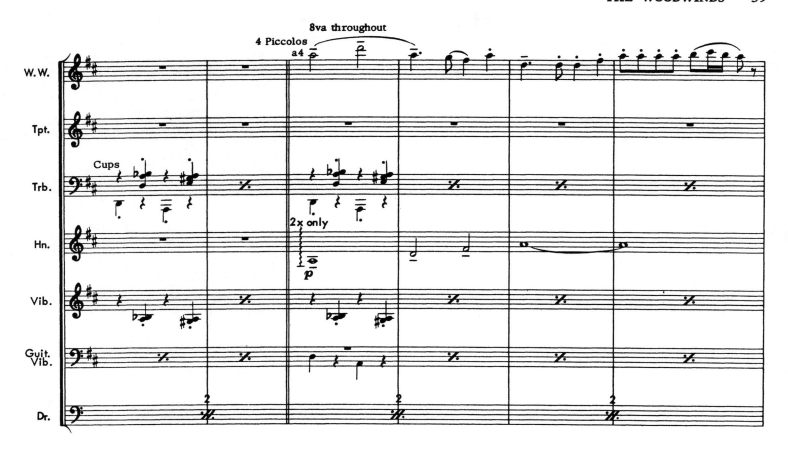

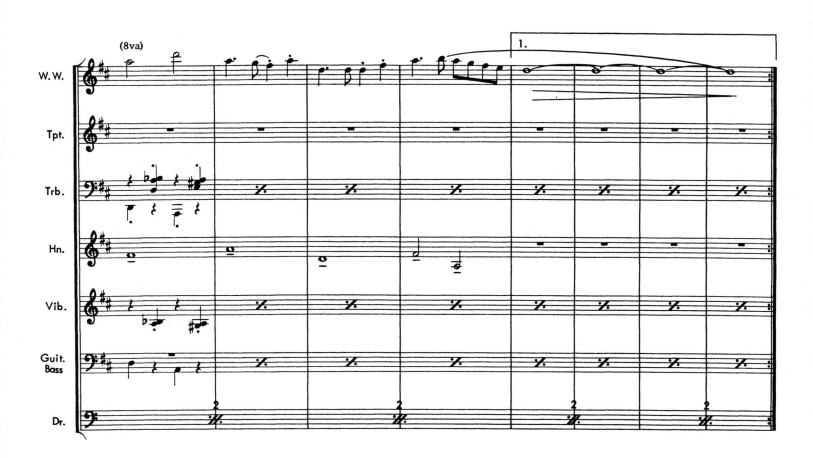

While we're dealing with thirds, let's take a look at the first statement of the melody in "Chime Time" (*Mr. Lucky*). Here we have two piccolos in thirds doubled an octave below by two oboes. The piccolo parts here could easily have been played by two flutes, since the range is perfect. However, the piccolo sound gives the tune a lighter and more buoyant feeling:

EXAMPLE 23   *CHIME TIME*   Side A, Band 2

One would hardly think of the piccolo as having the ability to "sing out" a lyrical melody. In "Softly" (*Mr. Lucky*) following Buddy Cole's plaintive organ solo, the four piccolos play in unison with the high violins. They add a clarity to the violins while not overpowering the basic string sound:

EXAMPLE 24   *SOFTLY*   Side A, Band 2

The C Flute

The C flute has long been a standard-bearer for the flute family. You will find that most reed sections have at least one or two available. It is an extremely good mixer, especially with other members of the woodwind family.

The flute requires no transposition and sounds where it is written:

EXAMPLE 25   *THE C FLUTE*

The "Mr. Lucky Theme" (*Mr. Lucky*) shows off the useful octave doubling of two flutes and two oboes. It occurs in the last eight bars of the first chorus. Two clarinets could be substituted for the oboes, creating a softer and less pointed over-all sound:

EXAMPLE 26   *MR. LUCKY*   Side A, Band 3

In "Tipsy" (*Mr. Lucky*) after the intro, the two flutes and two oboes play the theme in unison. This combination in this particular range has a peculiar nasal quality, quite oriental in character. The twelve-bar theme is then repeated with our four woodwinds playing an octave higher. In this range, note the unusual power and clarity of sound:

EXAMPLE 27   *TIPSY*   Side A, Band 3

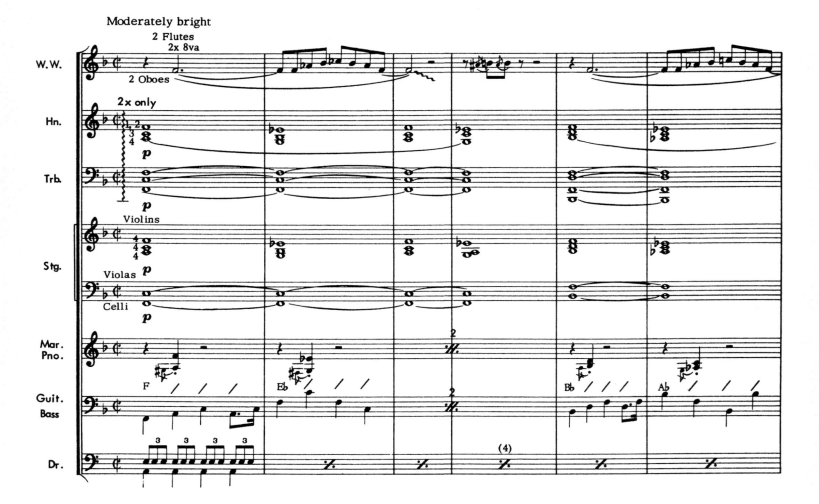

A comic effect is heard in the opening bar of "The Little Man Theme" .(*More Peter Gunn*), using minor seconds with two flutes on each part. The image of our "Little Man" is firmly established right from the down- beat:

EXAMPLE 28   *THE LITTLE MAN THEME*   Side A, Band 3

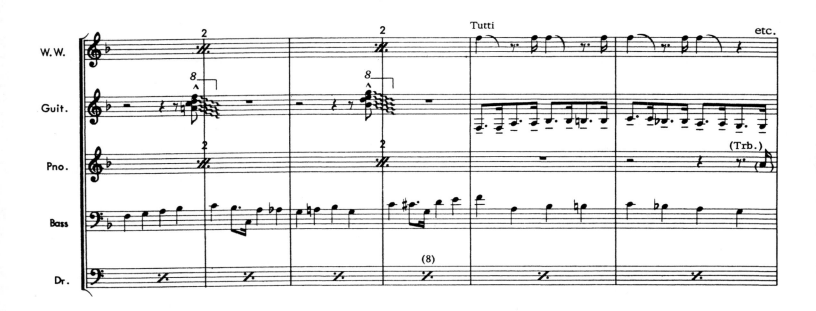

After the intro in "Odd Ball" (*More Peter Gunn*), four flutes take over, doubled by four trumpets in cup mutes an octave lower:

EXAMPLE 29   *ODD BALL*   Side A, Band 3

In tutti ensemble involving strings and brass the flute can help out by doubling the high lead string line. In the top half of its register it reinforces the violins.

The Alto Flute

The alto flute (G flute) has certainly come into its own. It is now practically a must that the flutist double on alto flute.

The instrument is built in G. The transposition is up a perfect fourth:

EXAMPLE 30   *THE ALTO FLUTE*

As a solo instrument, especially playing jazz, its range is often two and a half octaves. However, for written solos and section work the first octave and a half are the most effective. Its sound adds a new, dramatic dimension to the flute family.

Since the instrument is longer and has a larger bore than a C flute, it takes more wind to produce a sound. Sustained notes are fine, but don't get too many of them into a phrase without leaving some space to breathe.

A prime consideration is the use of the microphone to amplify the sound. The beautiful sound of the alto flute does not project very far unless helped out by amplification.

Our next example shows the four alto flutes in unison providing a springboard for Larry Bunker's driving vibraphone solo. The piece is "Blue Steel" (*More Peter Gunn*):

EXAMPLE 31   *BLUE STEEL*   Side B. Band 1

Turning to a ballad, "Joanna" (*More Peter Gunn*), we see the use of four alto flutes, first in unison and then spreading into a four-part background behind Dick Nash's lovely trombone solo:

EXAMPLE 32   *JOANNA*   Side B. Band 1

Midway through the "Little Man Theme" (*More Peter Gunn*) the four alto flutes provide a lightly swinging send-off for the marimba solo by Victor Feldman:

EXAMPLE 33   *THE LITTLE MAN THEME*   Side B, Band 1

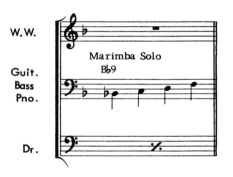

"A Cool Shade of Blue" (*The Mancini Touch*) starts off with an unusual ad lib alto flute intro by Ronnie Lang, followed by four bars of rhythm to get us into the mood for the opening melodic statement. Here we have our first encounter with the sax and flute in unison. In this case, two alto flutes are doubled by an alto sax. However, a single alto sax and a single alto flute provide one of the most workable of modern sounds. It has both coolness and body:

EXAMPLE 34 *A COOL SHADE OF BLUE*

Side B, Band 1

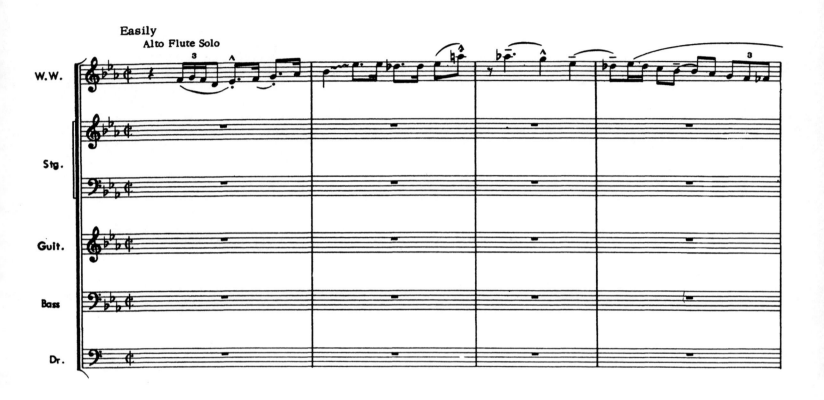

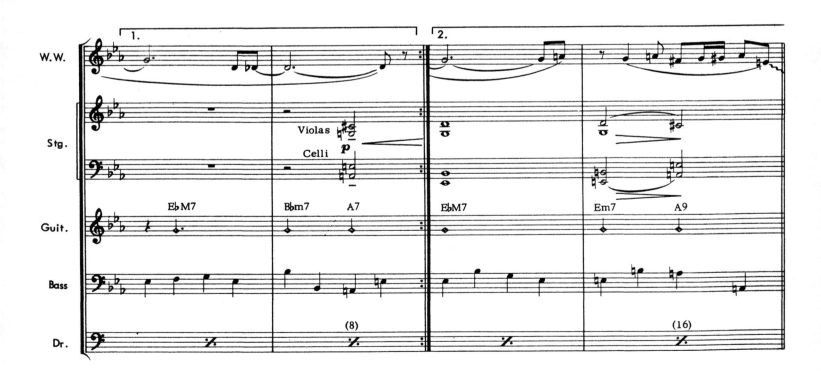

The Bass Flute

The "rare bird" of the flute family is an odd-looking bit of plumbing called the bass flute. Its strange appearance belies the fact that it has one of the most pleasing sounds in the entire orchestra. The bass flute is built in C and is written in the treble clef an octave above where it sounds:

EXAMPLE 35   *THE BASS FLUTE*

What we said about the alto flute being a windy instrument goes double for the bass flute. A tremendous amount of breath is needed to make a decent sound. Short notes or staccato passages are out of the question.

Recorded examples are a bit rare but we do have a few for illustration.

Four bass flutes were used in the first chorus of "The Blues" (*The Blues and the Beat*). Two microphones were set up with the men playing in very close to pick up this elusive sound:

EXAMPLE 36   *THE BLUES*

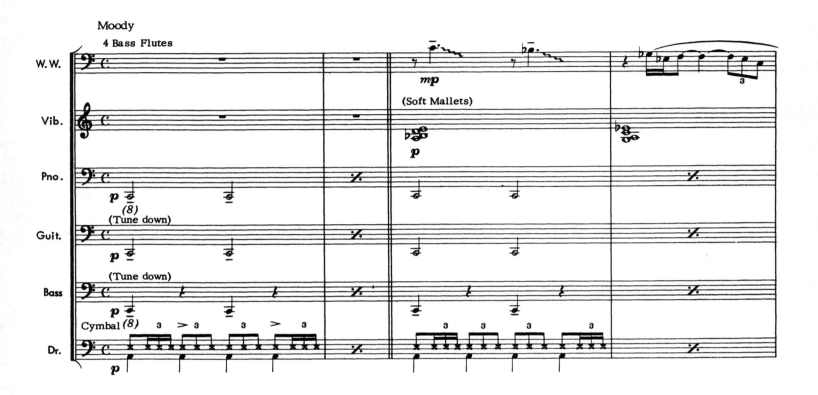

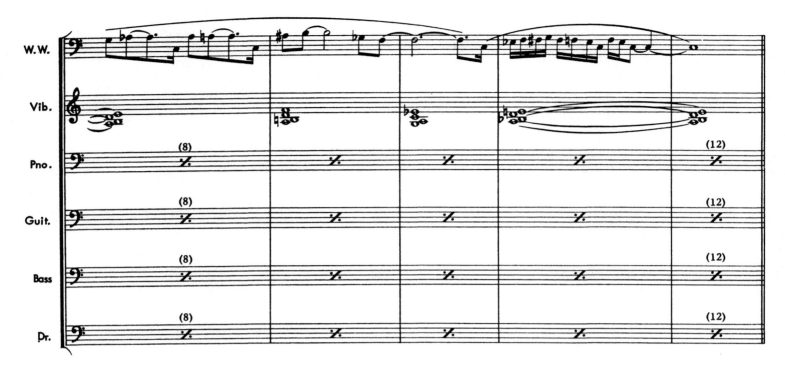

In the first woodwind entrance in "Floating Pad" (*Mr. Lucky*) we have two bass flutes doubled an octave lower by two bass clarinets and a bassoon. The effect is quite dark and moody:

EXAMPLE 37   *FLOATING PAD*   Side B, Band 2

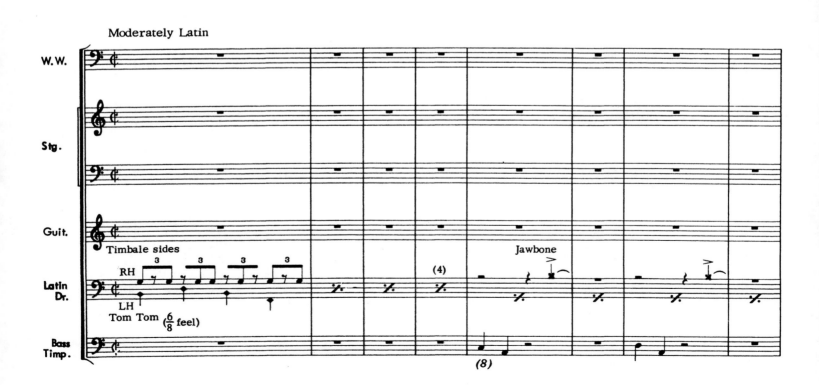

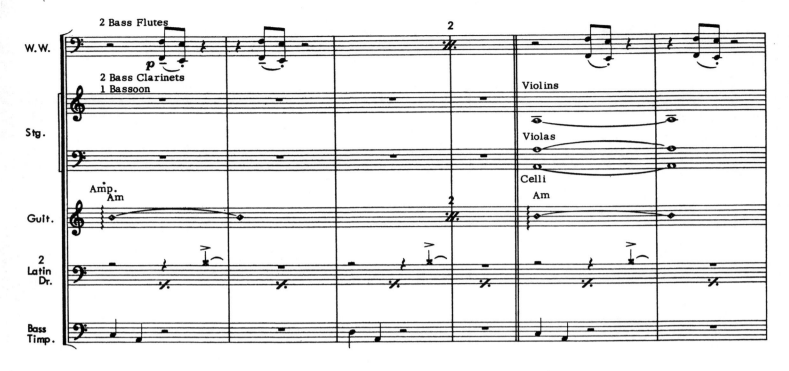

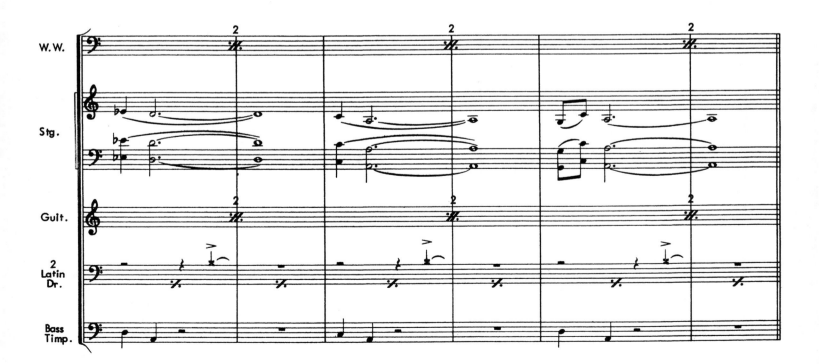

The Clarinet

The clarinet is an instrument of remarkable range, tone, flexibility, and agility. It probably rates second only to the violin in the number of things it can do well. Many pages could be written about its virtuoso capabilities, but I feel that its main value to the writer is in its application to section writing, both with other clarinets and with other members of the woodwind family.

You will find that every saxophone player, practically without exception, plays clarinet. This gives you a full section of four or five clarinets to start with. Within these four or five it is common to have at least one bass clarinet. As a section the clarinets are extremely useful for soft backgrounds. Tommy Dorsey used this color to wonderful advantage behind many of his trombone solos.

Being a B♭ instrument, the clarinet is transposed up one full tone. The bass clarinet is also in B♭ but is written in the treble clef up an octave and one full tone from where it sounds:

EXAMPLE 38   *THE B♭ CLARINET*

EXAMPLE 39   *THE B♭ BASS CLARINET*

Some of the newer bass clarinets are able to get down to the low D♭ and C. Check with your player before you write.

Using "Dreamsville" as our theme, let's examine a typical example of the clarinets used as background:

EXAMPLE 40   *DREAMSVILLE*

The problem we had earlier of using the extreme low end of the saxophone is non-existent in the clarinet family. In fact they are very comfortable down there and their sustaining power is excellent. On the other end of the stick we find that while the B♭ clarinet has relative ease throughout its range, the bass clarinet begins to get a pinched sound toward the end of its second octave.

While we're discussing the bass clarinet, let's take a look at an example of its use in a humorous vein. In "One-Eyed Cat" (*Mr. Lucky*), the rhythm section starts off, followed by the solo bassoon. He is joined by two bass clarinets playing along in unison until the cadence of the phrase. At that point they split into a trio. (This last bar serves to illustrate an exception to the rule of keeping the bass clarinet low. He goes a bit high here but to good effect.)

EXAMPLE 41   *ONE-EYED CAT*   Side B, Band 3

The clarinet is a very sociable fellow, especially when it comes to unison passages. It adds body no matter how it is used.

In the following examples the keys are changed to give the best possible sound to the instruments involved:

EXAMPLE 42

Unison:
Clarinet, Flute
Clarinet, Oboe
Clarinet, Flute, Oboe

EXAMPLE 43

In Octaves:
Flute

Clarinet

EXAMPLE 44

Oboe

Clarinet

EXAMPLE 45

Clarinet

Bass Clarinet
Bassoon

EXAMPLE 46

Flute

Oboe

Clarinet

EXAMPLE 47

Flute

Oboe

Clarinet

Bass Clarinet
Bassoon

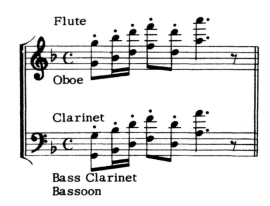

As you can see, the possibilities are quite extensive. Furthermore, all of these combinations work fine in slower and more melodic passages.

The Oboe

Moving over to the double reeds, we have first the oboe. It is a non-transposing instrument, written where it sounds:

EXAMPLE 48   *THE OBOE*

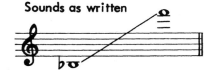

Except in the hands of a very capable player, the lowest three or four notes can sound quite strange. A good safe bottom would be the D one note up from middle C. The top octave is highly useful, especially for melodic passages. Unless your player is good, try not to write above the D below his high F.

The oboe can be quite a pixie because of its ability to rattle off staccato passages with ease.

In the second chorus of "March of the Cue Balls" (*Mr. Lucky*) we have good evidence of this. Two oboes and two piccolos were used:

Example 49   *MARCH OF THE CUE BALLS*   Side B, Band 4

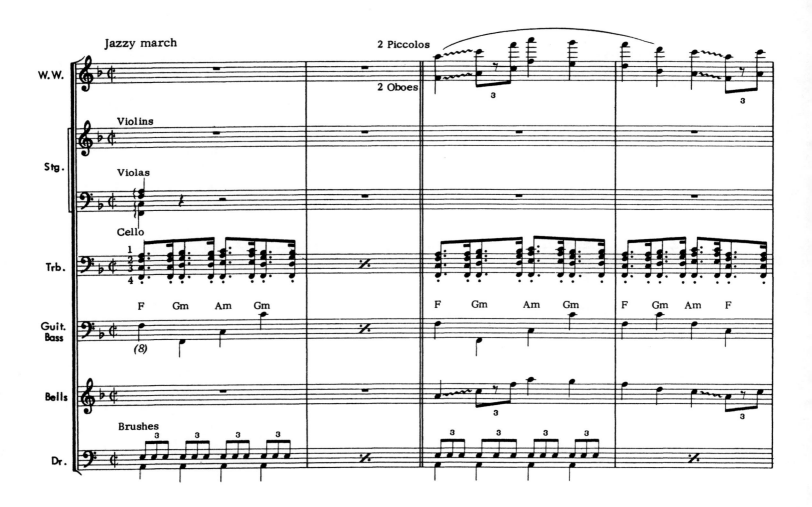

In the first release of "Lightly Latin" (*Mr. Lucky*) a somewhat frightened sound is uttered above the horns and trombones. Two oboes, two piccolos, and a xylophone are responsible for this:

EXAMPLE 50   *LIGHTLY LATIN*   Side B, Band 4

In the same number, following the organ solo, two oboes, two piccolos, and a bassoon take over the lead:

EXAMPLE 51   *LIGHTLY LATIN*   Side B, Band 4

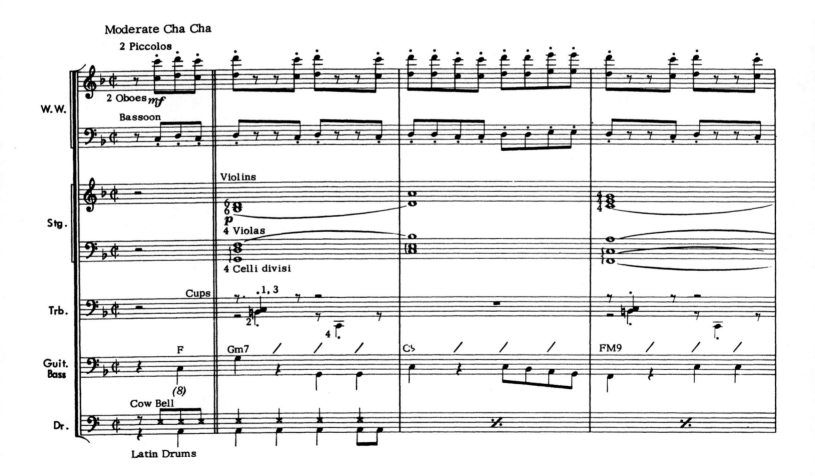

The intro and first eight bars of "Night Flower" (*Mr. Lucky*) show the oboes, flute, and piccolo in a light counter figure to the valve trombone solo. Two oboes do not overpower the flute and piccolo. Mixed woodwinds have a way of balancing within the section, whether they are divided or in unison:

EXAMPLE 52 *NIGHT FLOWER*

Side B, Band 4

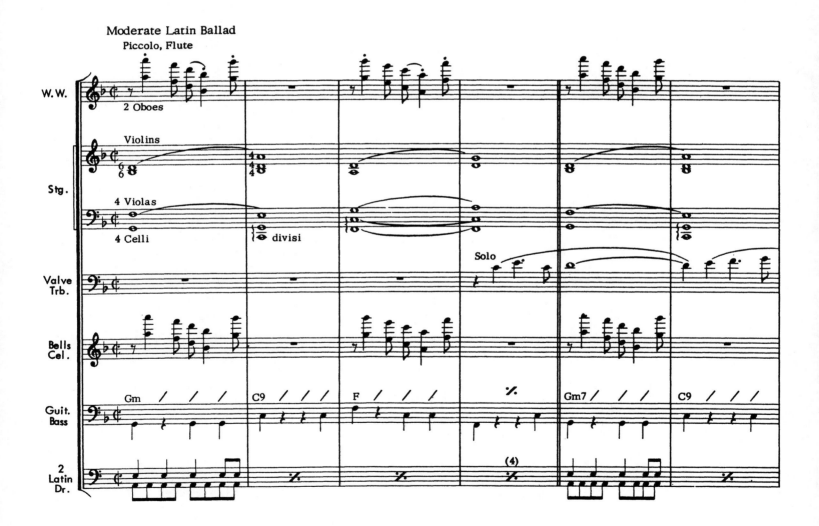

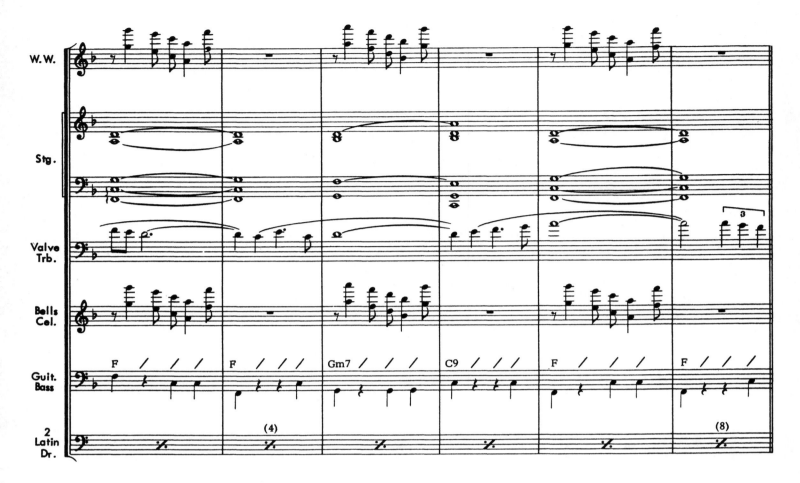

The English Horn

The English horn is built in F. The transposition is up a perfect fifth:

EXAMPLE 53   *THE ENGLISH HORN*

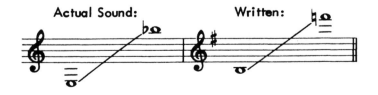

Here again we have the low note problem. The concert G above low E should put you on safe ground.

The English horn functions best within its first two octaves, especially in melodic passages.

Although not noted for such things, it can keep up pretty well with its brother, the oboe, when it comes to light, staccato passages.

The English horn should be kept in reserve for those special melodic passages. Its deep sound never fails to add a needed change of color so necessary to a well-balanced arrangement.

The Bassoon

As the piccolo is the comic of the high notes, the bassoon claims that distinction in the cellar. This by no means discounts his ability to caress a melody with a highly sensitive and expressive tone.

The bassoon is a non-transposing instrument and is written where it sounds in the bass clef:

EXAMPLE 54   *THE BASSOON*

The low notes on the instrument are easily played. The first two octaves and a perfect fifth (to the F above middle C) are the most practical and playable.

The bassoon blends beautifully with other woodwinds, especially in unison with the clarinet, the bass clarinet, the alto flute, the bass flute, or the English horn. Used as the bottom member in a divided woodwind passage it blends right in, no matter what the other instruments are.

Our first example shows the bassoon doing what no other instrument can quite duplicate. The opening statement of the melody in "One-Eyed Cat" (Ex. 41, page 63) immediately sets up the humorous mood of the whole piece.

"Lightly Latin" (*Mr. Lucky*) makes use of the low notes from the very beginning. Here they are employed in a kind of conversation with the other woodwinds:

EXAMPLE 55   *LIGHTLY LATIN*   Side C, Band 1

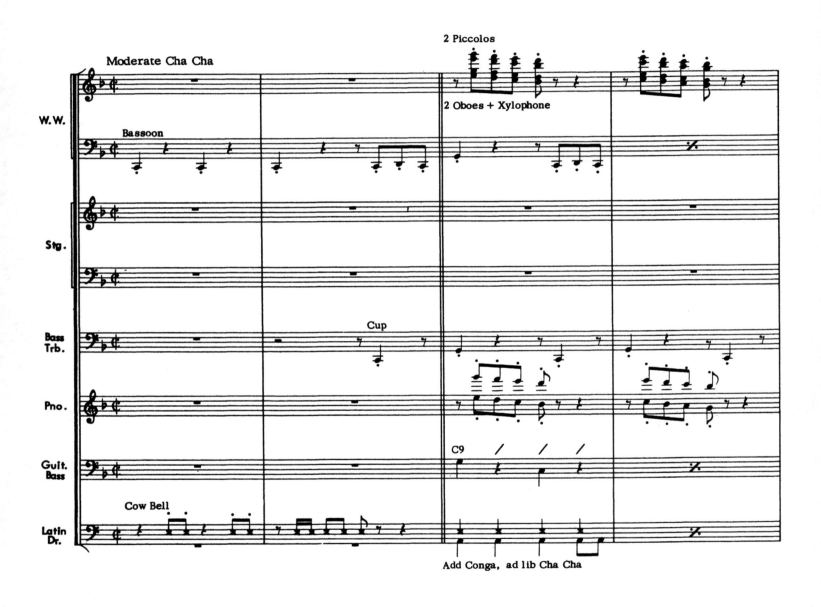

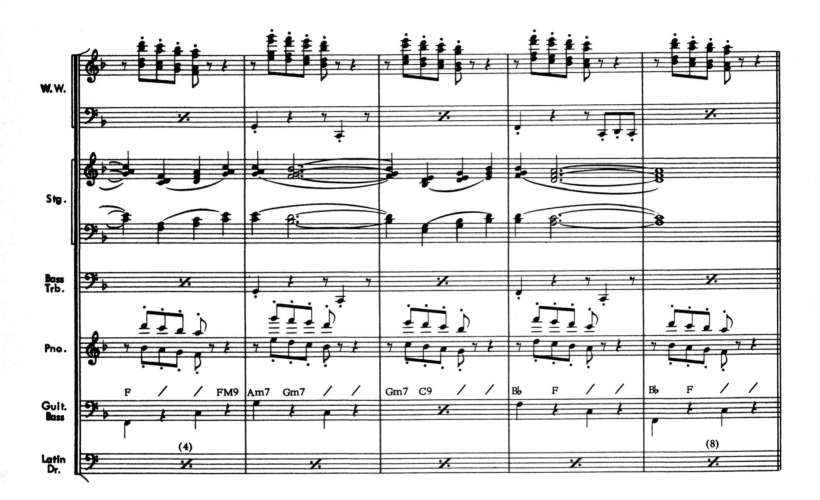

After the first release in "March of the Cue Balls" (*Mr. Lucky*) the bassoon and two bass clarinets take over the theme a tenth apart at first, then in thirds, and then back to tenths:

EXAMPLE 56   *MARCH OF THE CUE BALLS*   Side C, Band 1

Staccato passages are second nature to the bassoon. Scales and arpeggios can be executed with comparative ease. A word of advice, however: Leave a few breathing spaces in extended passages. May I point out once more the beautiful sound of which the bassoon is capable in melodic passages. For this purpose the middle to medium high range is best. All in all, despite its looks, the bassoon is a welcome and useful friend to the writer.

The Woodwind Ensemble

To set down and to discuss all the possibilities of the woodwind ensemble would fill a sizable volume. Fortunately, one of the facts of life in woodwind writing is that they all get along very well with each other. Just about any sensible combination of any number of woodwinds will result in a nicely balanced sound. The job of the writer is to know how to get the best possible combinations out of the instruments he has to work with. A knowledge of the best workable range of each instrument is your insurance for a good-sounding section.

A good example of an unusual combination can be found in the wood-wind passage that follows Don Fagerquist's delightful opening trumpet solo in "That's It and That's All (*Mr. Lucky*). Here we have three alto flutes, one clarinet, and a bassoon playing the lightly swinging passage:

EXAMPLE 57   *THAT'S IT AND THAT'S ALL*   Side C, Band 2

The same voicing is used in the introduction of "Chime Time" (*Mr. Lucky*):

EXAMPLE 58   *CHIME TIME*   Side C, Band 2

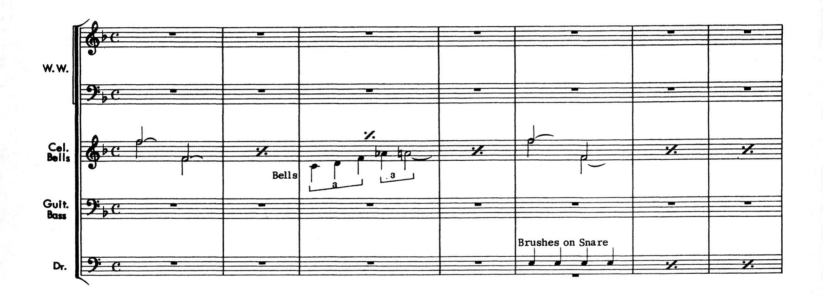

The use of flutes and clarinets together is quite practical, because these are the two main doubles in the sax section. It is extremely uncommon not to have at least one flute in a section. The flute playing lead over three or four clarinets is a very pretty sound. The main consideration here is not to write the flute too low. Keep him above his C in the staff (an octave above middle C). In this combination the first clarinet under the flute can go well into his high range without any trouble.

Using "Joanna" as our theme, here is a background consisting of one flute, three clarinets, and a bass clarinet:

EXAMPLE 59   *JOANNA*

Other combinations can be used for this same passage. In each case the bassoon can substitute for the bass clarinet:

1. flute/flute/clarinet/clarinet/bass clarinet (bassoon)
2. flute/oboe/clarinet/clarinet/bass clarinet (bassoon)
3. oboe/clarinet/clarinet/clarinet/bass clarinet (bassoon)
4. oboe/clarinet/clarinet/English horn/bass clarinet (bassoon)

It becomes obvious that the possibilities are numerous, pointing up again that the woodwinds do indeed get along well with each other.

Since our previous example was in the medium high range, let's look at the same number with a lower-pitched background.

The first group will consist of English horn or oboe (preferably English horn in this key)/clarinet/clarinet/clarinet/bass clarinet:

EXAMPLE 60   *JOANNA*

Some variations on that group:

1. oboe/English horn/clarinet/clarinet/bassoon
2. English horn/clarinet/clarinet/bass clarinet/bassoon
3. alto flute/clarinet/clarinet/bassoon/bass clarinet
4. clarinet/English horn/clarinet/bass clarinet/bassoon
5. English horn/alto flute/clarinet/bass clarinet/bassoon

Again we see that there are many possible combinations.

An interesting question comes up here. Who goes on the bottom, the bass clarinet or the bassoon? Normally the bassoon on the bottom is preferred, because it has a somewhat fatter sound. Another point is that the bassoon can go four notes lower than the bass clarinet, a big advantage in certain keys.

When you have an especially pretty counter melody as the lead voice in your background and you want to bring it out, a simple device can be applied. Have two instruments carry the lead counter line and your remaining voices fill the harmony. With two men on the second lead line, we have only three voices for the remaining harmony. We must now voice the chord for four voices instead of five. In the higher keys the C flute and oboe would be available for the top line:

EXAMPLE 61   *JOANNA*

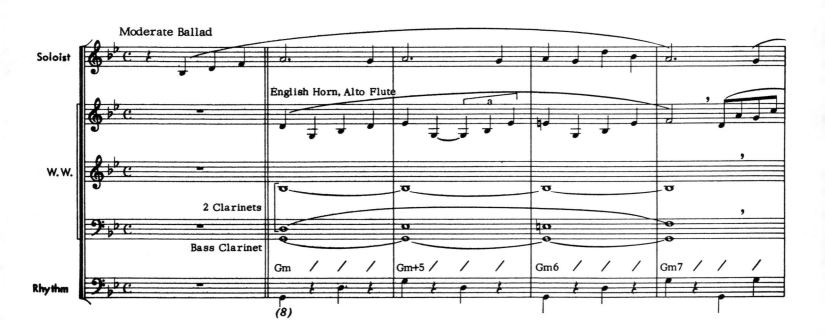

Other combinations:

Lead	Harmony
Lead	*Harmony*
1. Clarinet and alto flute	1. cl./cl./bass cl. (bassoon)
2. Clarinet and English horn	2. cl./cl./bass cl. (bassoon)
3. English horn and alto flute	3. cl./bassoon/bass cl.
4. Alto flute and bassoon	4. English horn/cl./bass cl.

The woodwind family presents an inexhaustible supply of colors. A thorough study of the capabilities and the limitations of each of its members will pay large dividends in interesting and colorful sounds.

The Brass

CHAPTER FOUR

The Brass

THE MODERN BRASS SECTION IS A HIGHLY MOBILE UNIT. ITS dynamic range is wide, going from a soft, full-bodied ballad sound to a double *forte* of utter violence.

The Trumpet

The trumpets are the most flexible members of the brass family. The *Peter Gunn* recording orchestra can boast of a "dream" section that includes Conrad Gozzo, Pete Candoli, Frank Beach, Joe Triscari, and Graham Young.

The trumpet is a Bb instrument. This calls for a transposition up one full tone:

EXAMPLE 62 *THE TRUMPET*

The range of the trumpet depends on the player, with some going up to the high F and then some. For purposes of practical writing the concert Bb, an octave and a minor seventh above middle C, is more realistic. Here, once more, be guided by the ability of your players. In unison, two, three, or four trumpets are an extremely powerful sound. The climax in "Fallout" (*Peter Gunn*) is driven home forcefully by two trumpets on the high lead and two trumpets an octave below. This device of using one or two trumpets an octave below the lead trumpets is a useful one. It gives a great deal of body and power to the line:

EXAMPLE 63   *FALLOUT*   Side C, Band 3

Trumpets in unison playing in the medium low register, with cup mutes or into hats, is a nice color for vocal or solo backgrounds. Into hats they sound best when playing with "no vibrato." (This is indicated on the parts as "N.V.") The sound is quite similar to that of a French horn. The trombones also use this quite often.

One word of advice: Use common sense when writing trumpet passages. Scoring them consistently high will eventually lead to disaster. No arrangement can sound to best advantage when the trumpets are straining. Give them a break and you will find that your arrangements are more **playable** and better-sounding.

The Trombone

The slide trombone is written where it sounds in the bass clef and requires no transposition:

EXAMPLE 64   *THE TROMBONE*

Any note from that top Bb to the F above is for experts only.
There are also a few low pedal notes available for special effects:

EXAMPLE 65   *TROMBONE PEDAL NOTES*

The easiest of these is the Bb. It is played in the first position and can be relied upon. Don't expect anything on the delicate side from these pedal notes. They are big, fat sounds that must be played out to be effective.

The trombone comes with a couple of built-in hazards in the form of the low E♮ and the B♮ a fifth above. These two notes must be played in the seventh position, thus creating a physical problem in getting to and from notes played in the first and second positions. The only way to get from a low B♮ to the Bb below is to go from the seventh position to the first. If the change is fast it is difficult even for the best of players. Another point about that seventh position: These notes are a bit difficult to sustain and control. Unless a bass trombone is available to you, be very careful how you handle your low man.

The bass trombone is becoming common and is a most welcome addition to the brasses. It adds quite a few notes to the bottom of the section. It is also written where it sounds:

EXAMPLE 66   *THE BASS TROMBONE*

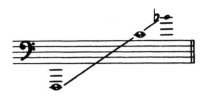

Notes with which a tenor trombone would have to struggle come easily for the bass trombone. Since it takes quite a bit of wind to blow the horn, make a special effort to find places for the player to breathe in sustained passages.

"A Cool Shade of Blue" (*The Mancini Touch*) shows two good basic possibilities of the trombone section. After the strings play the release of the first chorus, the trombones (Dick Nash, Jimmy Priddy, Johnny Halliburton, and Karl De Karske) take over the last eight bars of the chorus. The range here is perfect for this type of easygoing number:

EXAMPLE 67   *A COOL SHADE OF BLUE*   Side C, Band 4

Later in the same piece the cup-muted trombones play a unison figure leading into the guitar solo. We have two on a higher line and two doubling an octave below:

EXAMPLE 68   *A COOL SHADE OF BLUE*   Side C, Band 4

One of the prettiest of sounds is the trombone section playing background to a solo or vocal. In the second release of "Dreamsville" (*Peter Gunn*), our section lays down a velvet carpet for Ted Nash's wistful alto sax solo:

EXAMPLE 69 *DREAMSVILLE*   Side C. Band 4

The previous example was a background using close voicing. The trombones also can form a rich, organ-type of backing when written in open voicing. "Joanna" (*More Peter Gunn*) shows this behind the four-horn unison lead, the last eight bars of the first chorus:

EXAMPLE 70   *JOANNA*   Side C, Band 4

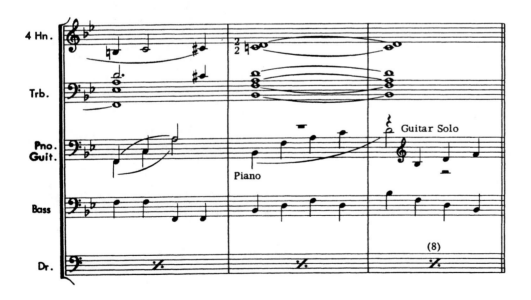

The trombones can be very funny fellows on occasion. The introduction of "Timothy" (Ex. 22, page 38) has them pumping away at the humorous marching figure, making fine contrast to the four piccolos who enter shortly after with the theme.

Those built-in hazards we spoke of earlier, the seventh position for the low E and B, now become blessings. Because of this the trombone is capable of an effect no other wind instrument can duplicate: the true glissando. The two longest glisses can be made from the low E♮ (seventh position) to the B♭ above (first position), and from the next B♮ (seventh position) to the F above (first position):

EXAMPLE 71   *TROMBONE GLISSANDO*

They also work fine an octave higher. Of course, you can gliss to and from any of the notes in between.

Some parting words: Use the same restraint in writing for trombones that you do for your trumpets. Don't get them consistently high. The trombones shouldn't be babied too much when it comes to moving passages. They get around pretty well. Ample proof of this can be found in the Sousa marches.

The French Horn

The French horn has surely come into its own in the jazz and popular field. If any instrument ever had a naturally cool sound, this is it. The only problem here is to find players who can sit in and phrase with the rest of the brass section.

The *Peter Gunn* orchestra is fortunate in having four such men led by the incomparable Vincent De Rosa. John Graas, John Cave, and Richard ·Perissi round out the section.

The most widely used French horn is built in F. A transposition up a perfect fifth is necessary:

EXAMPLE 72   *THE FRENCH HORN*

The best usable range extends from the low concert F in the bass clef to the C or D an octave above middle C. The horn can play long, sustained passages beautifully.

A carry-over from legitimate notation is the practice of omitting the key signature and writing in all of the accidentals. Although this is in common use today, you do have the option of using key signatures.

The ninth bar of the "Mr. Lucky Theme" (*Mr. Lucky*) shows how effective unison horns can be:

EXAMPLE 73   *MR. LUCKY THEME*   Side C, Band 5

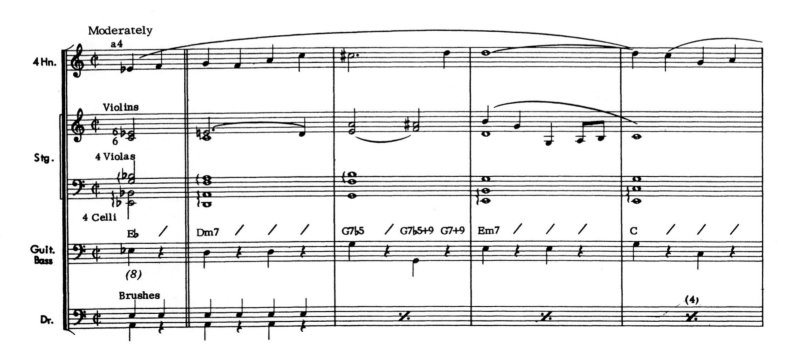

A good special effect, the lipped gliss, is found in the "Peter Gunn Theme" (*Peter Gunn*) behind the wailing alto sax solo. This is very high and difficult for the horns:

EXAMPLE 74   *PETER GUNN*   Side C, Band 5

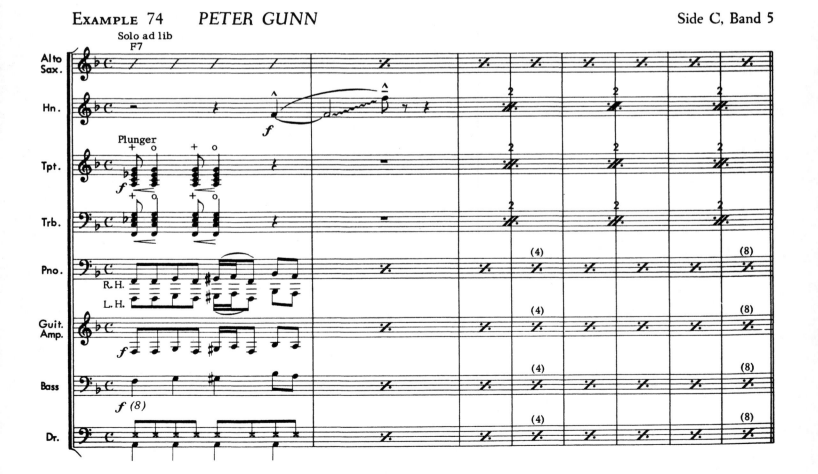

The intro and first eight bars of "Softly" (*Mr. Lucky*) has the horns in a very relaxed range playing the unison counter line, while the trombones form the basic harmony. This is very easily played and extremely effective:

EXAMPLE 75   *SOFTLY*   Side C, Band 5

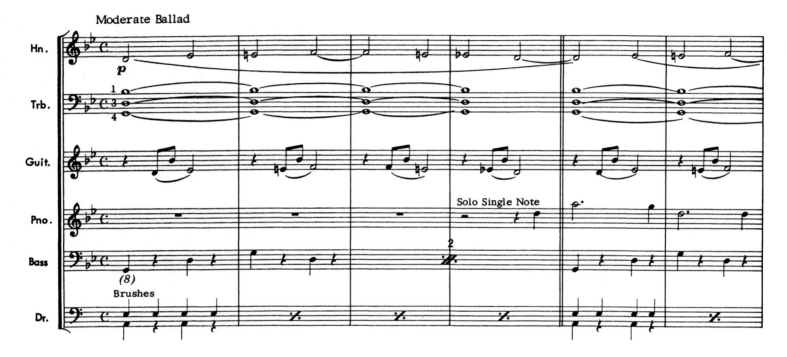

By putting his hand into the bell of his horn the player can produce a sound that is strained and muffled. This is called "stopped" and is indicated by a "+" above the note you wish stopped. He can also play with his hand only half in. This is indicated by a "½+" above the note. Save this effect for your more dramatic writing.

The union of horns and trombones is a sound that has been used quite freely in the *Peter Gunn* and *Mr. Lucky* music. It is confined almost exclusively to sustained and pretty passages. Breathing and phrasing are the big considerations here. Although the horns can play extended passages fairly well, the low trombones cannot. Plan your phrasing with this in mind.

The first entrance of the horns and trombones in "Dreamsville" (*Peter Gunn*) is typical of this color:

EXAMPLE 76　　*DREAMSVILLE*　　　　　　　　　　　Side C, Band 5

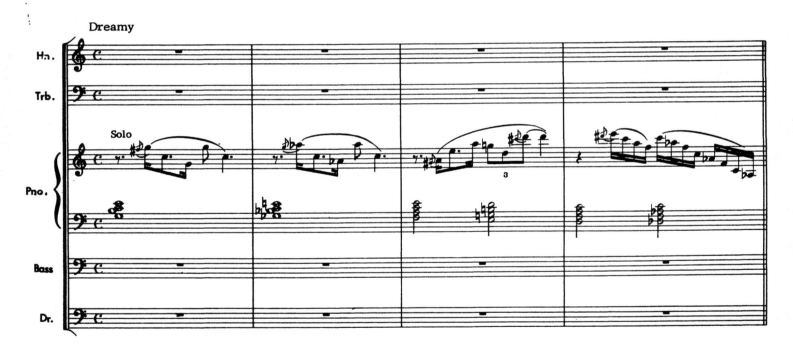

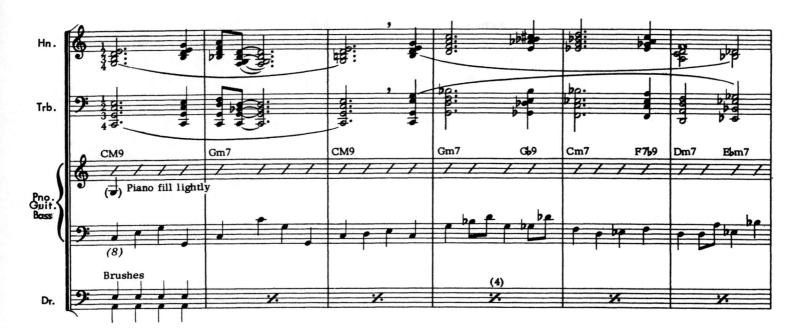

Notice that in the last two notes of the first ending, the first and second horns are doubling the lead. This is common and perfectly permissible. When the lead gets too low it can be given extra body in this manner without upsetting the over-all balance.

I should point out, in passing, that the low part in the Trombone Quartet can be assigned to a Tuba; if you have three Trombones (Tenor, Tenor and Bass). This makes the Bass Trombonist's life a bit easier.

Looking back to the example we used for the trumpets, "Fallout" (Ex. 63, page 100), we see that in *forte* chords and passages it becomes imperative that we put two horns on each note. A four-note horn chord here would be helplessly lost between the high trumpets and the low trombones playing *forte*.

For the sake of the band that has only one French horn, let's see how we can best utilize his talents.

The following example, "Dreamsville" again, has the horn playing lead over four trombones. This same passage can be applied to horn over four saxes or horn over four clarinets. In each case the section under the horn plays with no vibrato.

EXAMPLE 77   *DREAMSVILLE*

One or two horns can also be put to good use doubling just about anything in a unison line, whether it be a *forte* passage with the brass or a softer, more subtle line with saxes, woodwinds, strings, or trombones. The horn adds its own special color to the over-all sound.

The Tuba

The tuba is making a successful bid to become part of the danceband brass family, obviously becoming bored with doubling the bass drum for a living. Here is an instrument that has much to offer. It is of course written in the bass clef:

EXAMPLE 78   *THE TUBA*

The tuba can move well, making it valuable on the bottom of a moving brass section. Here again breath is a prime consideration in low, sustained passages. Treat it in the same way you would the bass trombone. Low unisons with the tuba doubling the bass trombone or the tuba doubling the low trombone an octave lower are powerful and dramatic. If you have a good tuba player available, put him to work.

The Brass Ensemble

Our first look at the brass section is "Session at Pete's Pad" (*Peter Gunn*). After Johnny Williams' gracefully swinging piano introduction our eight brass enter in a passage voiced on the low side. We see here just how effective the brass can be while taking it easy. The third and fourth trumpets are quite low, but since everyone is playing easy, they hold their own and are not lost:

EXAMPLE 79   *SESSION AT PETE'S PAD*   Side D, Band 1

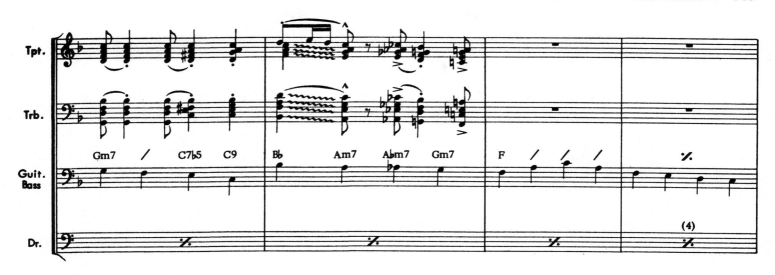

Since eight brass are not common in most bands, here is the same passage scored for several smaller sections:

EXAMPLE 80   *SESSION AT PETE'S PAD*

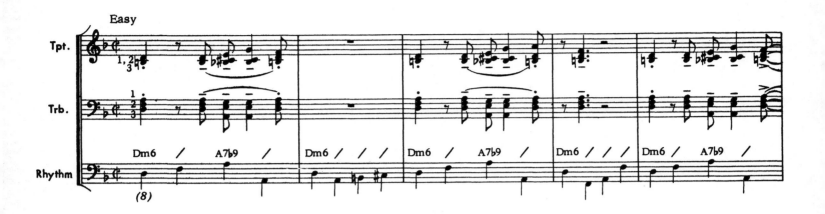

EXAMPLE 81   *SESSION AT PETE'S PAD*

EXAMPLE 82 *SESSION AT PETE'S PAD*

Turning to a ballad, "Blues for Mother's" (*More Peter Gunn*), the brass take over going into the last eight bars of the first chorus. Note that the trombones remain stationary while the trumpets weave in and out. The resultant doubling of notes in no way disturbs the over-all balance:

EXAMPLE 83   *BLUES FOR MOTHER'S*   Side D, Band 1

EXAMPLE 84   *BLUES FOR MOTHER'S*

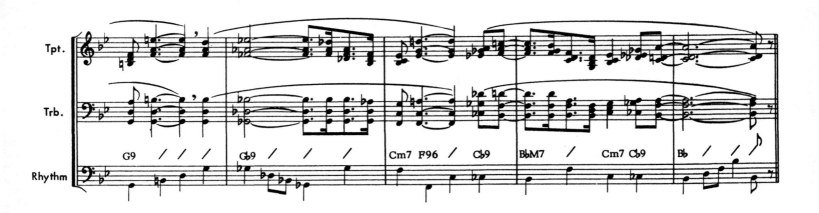

EXAMPLE 85   *BLUES FOR MOTHER'S*

EXAMPLE 86   *BLUES FOR MOTHER'S*

Led by Conrad Gozzo's brilliant lead trumpet, an especially full and majestic-sounding brass passage can be found in "Joanna" (*More Peter Gunn*), just after the horns have stated the last eight bars of the first chorus. This is strictly for eight brass and should not be attempted with less:

EXAMPLE 87   *JOANNA*   Side D, Band 1

Under the piccolos playing in thirds in the first release of "Timothy" (Ex. 22, page 38), the muted brass bite off fill-in figures. In practically any range these are effective. The same passage for:

EXAMPLE 88   *TIMOTHY*

EXAMPLE 89   *TIMOTHY*

EXAMPLE 90   *TIMOTHY*

Permit us a generalization at this point. Close, tight voicing makes for a more swinging feel in fast and medium tempoed numbers. Widespread voicing in these tempos has a leaden effect and tends to bog down the whole band.

By adding the French horns to the trumpets and trombones, the "Peter Gunn Theme" (*Peter Gunn*) clearly shows the horns' relation to the rest of the section. Here they are placed practically in the middle of the section, doubling the fourth trumpet and the first three trombones. Once more, be assured that the over-all balance of the section is not disrupted by this doubling. There is no definite rule to follow when using the horns in this manner. Put them in a good, solid register and make them well-sounding within themselves:

EXAMPLE 91   *PETER GUNN*   Side D, Band 2

The last eight bars of the first chorus of "Dreamsville" (*Peter Gunn*) starts off with the four trombones, who are then joined by the rest of the brass in a rich, full-sounding ensemble. The horns start, doubling the four trumpets, but then drop to a lower position to reinforce the counter harmonies. They return to their original positions (doubling the trumpets) and then finish out the phrase with the trombones:

EXAMPLE 92   *DREAMSVILLE*

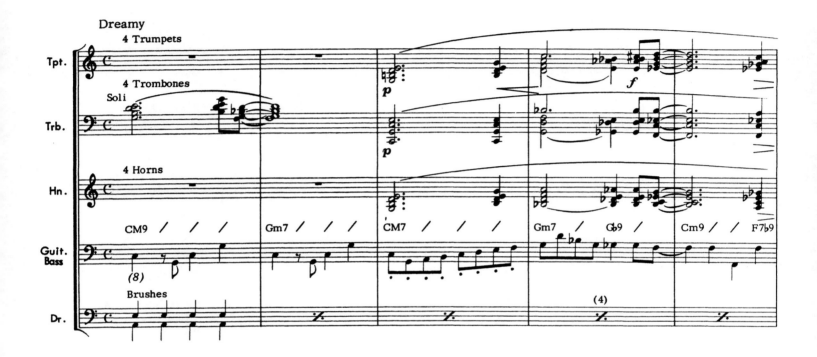

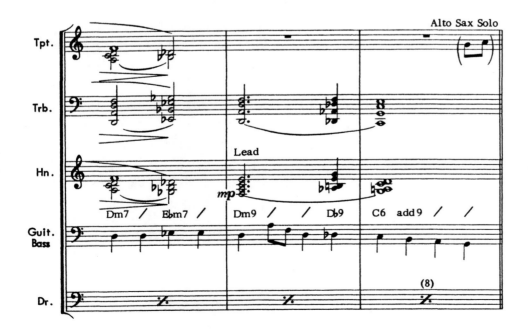

In smaller sections the problem of what to do with one or two French horns becomes more evident. We are no longer concerned with merely doubling the horns with the other brass. Now each voice in the chord must count. The most effective rule here is to treat your horn (or horns) as an extension of your trumpets. In other words, sandwich them between your trumpets and trombones. This type of voicing works best in the softer ballads.

When the brass are really blowing loud, fast, and hard, the horns (or horn) should go back to their doubling role, or they should be left out. However, if your men have good jazz conception and can keep up with the rest of the brass, by all means let them blow.

Brass Mutes

A word about mutes before we leave the brasses. There are three basic mutes in general use: the cup mute; the straight mute; and the Harmon or copper mute. Only the first two are available to the French horn.

The cup mute is the softest of the trio, enabling it to blend well with the woodwinds. A very soft and velvety sound can be achieved by stuffing a handkerchief around the inside of the mute before inserting it into the instrument. Cups have a good bite to them when played *forte*.

The straight mute (brass mute) creates a piercing, biting sound that is best applied to moderate and up-tempo numbers. This mute can also be mixed in with the woodwinds to good effect, mostly in sharp, rhythmic figures.

The Harmon mute has a kind of chilling, thin sound that is wonderful for "strange" effects. It is built with a nozzle that can be pulled in or out as desired. With the nozzle entirely out it produces a filtered, hollow sound.

One word of caution about using mutes in trumpets. Keep them in a medium or medium high range. Muted trumpets have a tendency to play out of tune when they are written too low. Stay above middle C with your lower man.

Although it is not considered a mute, the plunger can be placed in this general category. The plunger effect is usually produced by the rubber end of a plumber's aid. A plastic cup is also available. The third and least effective means is the hand. The "Peter Gunn Theme" (Ex. 74, page 108) shows this device in action. The stopped notes are marked "+" and the open ones "O".

Since it takes a bit of time to put a mute in or take it out, leave the brass at least a few bars to maneuver.

Brass and Saxophone Ensemble

The most effective and downright thrilling of sounds is that of all of the wind instruments playing an ensemble passage. It is here that an orchestra (and the arranger) shows its real class and ability.

Setting the French horns aside, let's get to the practical work of combining the brass and the saxes into a solid, moving group. In a medium-tempoed groove, "The Beat" (*The Blues and the Beat*) is a typical example. Our ensemble follows the trumpet solo. In this particular case the trumpet, who has just finished his solo, is excused from the ensemble for the first eight bars, joining in later on the second eight. The reason for this is simple. Four trumpets weren't at all necessary for the passage, so why not let the soloist rest for a bit? Going into a solo from an ensemble, it is also wise to leave your soloist out of the preceding action. In other words, give him time to wind up or unwind, as the case may be.

In this example the brass are the body of the ensemble. Note that the four saxes are a solid, complete unit in themselves. There is no rule as to who is doubled by whom. Just make sure that the saxes are in a good-sounding register. Incidentally, had we used a fifth baritone sax here, he would have doubled the bass trombone:

EXAMPLE 93   *THE BEAT*   Side D, Band 2

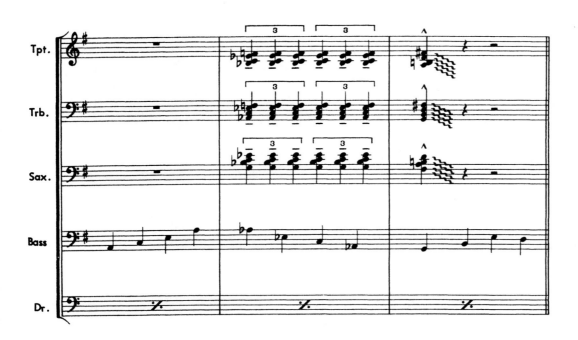

Let's do the first eight bars of this passage for two smaller groups. First,
3 trumpets/2 trombones/4 saxes (A A T B):

EXAMPLE 94   *THE BEAT*

Next, 2 trumpets/1 trombone/3 saxes (A A T). Notice that our trombone drops down and becomes the bass voice:

EXAMPLE 95   *THE BEAT*

A thing of beauty is a full-bodied, deeply voiced ballad ensemble. Again using "Blues for Mother's" as our example, let's add five saxes (A A T T B) to our original eight brass. The saxes again are a very sonorous group within themselves:

EXAMPLE 96   *BLUES FOR MOTHER'S*

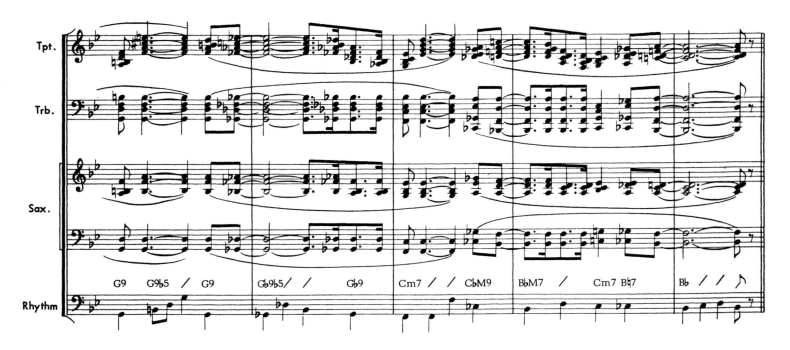

The same passage for 3 trumpets/3 trombones/4 saxes (A A T B):

EXAMPLE 97   *BLUES FOR MOTHER'S*

For 3 trumpets/2 trombones/4 saxes (A A T B):

EXAMPLE 98   *BLUES FOR MOTHER'S*

Next, for 2 trumpets/1 trombone/3 saxes (A A T):

EXAMPLE 99   *BLUES FOR MOTHER'S*

Finally, we have an up-tempoed, tightly voiced, swinging ensemble for 4 trumpets/4 trombones/5 saxes. Depth of voicing gives way to rhythmic drive:

EXAMPLE 100

Ensemble writing should be given much time and practice. It is here that the writer's talents are really put to the test. An ill-conceived ensemble can dissipate any emotion or momentum that you are trying to build. Here is one time that the soloist or singer need not be considered, the one time that the writer can step to the front.

Show and
Act Music

CHAPTER FIVE

Show and Act Music

EVERY ARRANGER IS CALLED UPON FROM TIME TO TIME TO write for various types of acts. The order is always the same: write for fifteen men—but it must be playable for six. This, of course, limits the writer enormously.

Since the score will often be played by smaller groups, all of the intros, endings, and fill-ins should be written for ensemble orchestra.

The first step is to write a solid trio for two trumpets and one trombone:

EXAMPLE 101

Next, add three saxes (A A T). The big advantage with this type of voicing is that it will sound well with just one trumpet and three saxes:

EXAMPLE 102

The third step is to fill in your remaining voices. Unlikely intervals may result but this is unavoidable:

EXAMPLE 103

Divided saxes are a problem, since you will end up with three or less in most cases. The use of unison saxes remedies this situation greatly.

In show music the piano part is usually a three-line part on the order of a simplified conductor's score. The top staff contains your lead and important band fills and figures. The bottom two staves are the regular part with one difference from what we've been doing in this book: the right-hand chords are written out. These chords should be kept in the area of middle C. If the arrangement is a busy one the band figures can be put in the second (right-hand piano) staff.

This particular part is not laid out in this form in your score. Write only the two-stave part and let the copyist make up the piano-conductor part later (poor cats who can't afford copyists notwithstanding).

All this is a purely functional format and has some obvious shortcomings. With a bit of probing, in some cases you will come up with little reinforcements that will give more depth to your voicings. But always remember that the score must serve the purposes of any size group that plays it.

The Rhythm Section

CHAPTER SIX

The Rhythm Section

Our present-day rhythm section usually includes the piano, the guitar, the bass, and drums. Some jazz groups have eliminated the guitar, proving that the bass and drums are perfectly capable of propelling the beat by themselves.

Another approach is the Count Basie rhythm sound. Here we have the bass and drums joined by the unamplified rhythm guitar. This is the style used most often by the big bands. The piano is present but is not actually contributing to the basic job of making rhythm.

The *Peter Gunn* orchestra has some of the finest rhythm men available: On drums, Jack Sperling or Shelley Manne; bass, Rolly Bundock or Red Mitchell; guitar, Bob Bain; vibes, Larry Bunker or Victor Feldman; and piano, Johnny Williams.

The Piano

Our first subject in the rhythm section is the acoustic piano. The normally accepted method of writing the piano part is to put the guitar chord symbols in the right hand and the bass line in the left hand. Sometimes these two are condensed into a single bass-clef staff. In dance orchestra writing the chords are seldom written out. No pianist takes his part literally. It serves only as a guide.

In recent years, we have had an "invasion of the Keyboards." The Rhodes Electric Piano and the Electric Organ have lead us into the world of the synthesizer—a world that is forever widening.

An exception to this is the society band field. The piano definitely becomes an important part of the rhythm section. Here the rhythm section usually plays a two-beat pattern. This means that the bass and the piano left hand play the bass line on the first and third beats only, and the piano right hand plays the second and fourth beats only. The right hand is generally written out, but chord symbols can be used.

In vocal background arrangements it is a most useful idea to cue the voice in the piano part. Many times the singer will want to run over an unfamiliar tune with the piano alone.

Aside from its obvious solo and fill-in talents, the piano is an excellent reinforcer. It can be used in any range to add color to the rest of the orchestra.

The ostinato bass line in the "Peter Gunn Theme" (Ex. 1, page 2), while basically a guitar figure, is given added power and drive by the piano.

In a previous example, "Fallout" (Ex. 63, page 100), the piano adds a percussive touch to the horn and trombone chords.

In the "Little Man Theme" (Ex. 28, page 49) a bit of color is added to the flutes.

The third bar of "Tipsy" (*Mr. Lucky*) has the piano and marimba starting the rhythmic pattern in a humorous vein:

EXAMPLE 104   *TIPSY*   Side D, Band 3

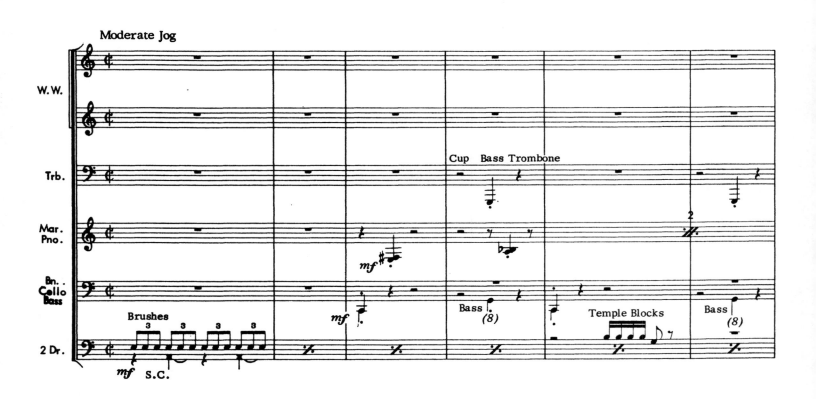

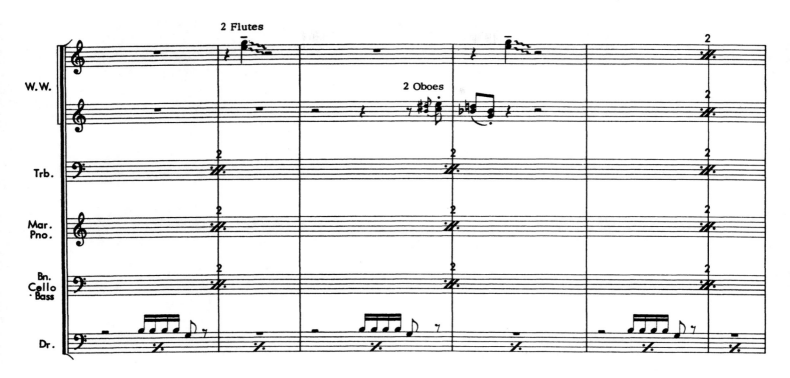

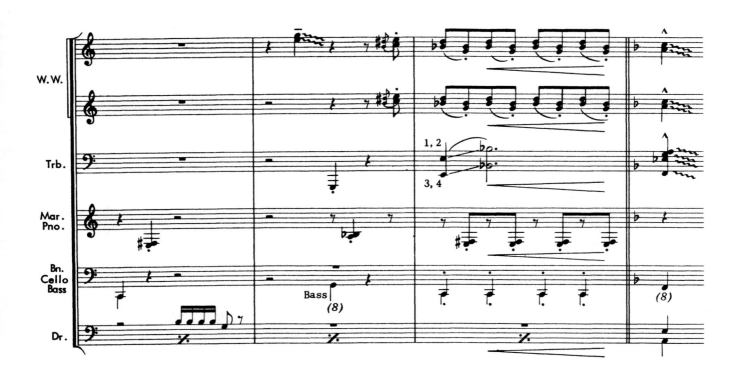

The possibilities of this kind of coloration are endless. A little extra thought in this direction will result in some very refreshing sounds.

The Celesta

While it is not very often seen on the bandstand, the celesta is available in every recording studio.

It is written one octave lower than it sounds:

EXAMPLE 105   *THE CELESTA*

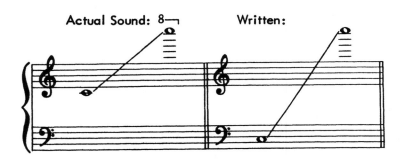

In somewhat the same manner as was discussed in our piano section, the celesta can be very effective when used to double other instruments, especially woodwinds and mallet percussion.

Looking back to "Night Flower" (Ex. 52, page 79), we see the celesta playing along in unison with the woodwinds. It adds a charming flavor to the figure.

"Chime Time" (Ex. 58, page 88) starts with the bells and the celesta in unison.

The last eight bars of the first chorus of "Blue Satin" (*Mr. Lucky*) have the celesta, the bells, and the vibes in unison, a good contrast to the incoming organ solo:

EXAMPLE 106   *BLUE SATIN*

Side D, Band 3

The celesta is wonderful for a delicate dash of color now and then.

The Guitar

The guitar is built in C and is written an octave above where it sounds:

EXAMPLE 107   *THE GUITAR*

Rhythm guitar is written:

EXAMPLE 108

If you should want a particular note voiced as the lead in a chord, write it:

EXAMPLE 109

Leave the range, inversion, and voicing of the chord up to the player. This is a no-man's-land for someone who doesn't play the instrument.

Most guitarists come prepared for anything. They have both an amplified guitar and an unamplified rhythm guitar (Spanish). The definitive example of the unamplified rhythm guitar can be found with Freddie Green of the Count Basie band. The true guitar sound blends perfectly with the drums and bass, giving the illusion of a single rhythm instrument.

Normally you cannot turn the power off in an amplified guitar and expect it to sound like a normal Spanish guitar. The instrument is built differently and cannot perform with the power off. This means, of course, that if you want to go from one to the other, you must switch instruments. This takes a bit of time, so leave at least eight bars rest for the player to change. However, there are some guitars built that can do both.

The amplified guitar is a formidable addition to any group. The quality of the sound goes from soft and delicate to downright raucous. The player has complete control of his high and low frequencies, much as you would on one of the better hi-fi rigs. Since the possibilities are practically infinite, the best sound for your particular need can only be achieved by experimentation. There is no way to notate exactly what you want.

The raucous sound we mentioned can be found in "The Peter Gunn Theme" (Ex. 1, page 2). Bob Bain's guitar is the basic, driving force.

Some amplified guitars have another device that is useful: the controlled vibrato. If your man has this on his instrument, he has complete control of his vibrato, ranging from very slow to very fast. "Spook" (Ex. 10, page 16) shows this off to fine advantage. It's quite a nervous sound.

The glissando is a practical device that the guitar does well. Single notes or chords, either up or down, can be handled with ease. Before you write, check to make sure that your glissando can be played without crossing strings. Otherwise it is impossible. The "Little Man Theme" (Ex. 28, page 49) shows the descending chordal gliss.

In the coda of "Goofin' at the Coffee House" (*More Peter Gunn*), the single note gliss is used:

EXAMPLE 110   *GOOFIN' AT THE COFFEE HOUSE*   Side D, Band 4

The last two bars of the previous example bring up an interesting situation. The guitar, the vibes, the piano, and the bass form an ensemble of their own. The vibes are on the upper two notes, the guitar on the next three, the piano consolidates the sound, and the bass holds down the bottom.

The last three bars of "A Quiet Gass" (*More Peter Gunn*) also show this off to great advantage:

EXAMPLE 111   *A QUIET GASS*   Side D, Band 4

"Joanna" (Ex. 32, page 52) has the guitar on the pretty side, doubling the piano in the accompaniment.

"Softly" (Ex. 75, page 109) is somewhat the same pattern. Here the guitar carries the accompaniment alone unamplified.

The amplified guitar is very important to smaller groups because of its ability to "feed" soloists with an infinite variety of sounds and patterns. The term "feed" is a common jazz expression for backing up a soloist. "Comping" is another term meaning the same thing. This "backing up" is not written out. The player uses his regular chord symbol part as a guide, in much the same way that the piano does.

For a special effect, the low E string can be tuned down as far as the C below. This has to be done before the piece starts so that the string can be tuned correctly. Don't expect the player to do anything else later in the number involving that E string because tuning it down throws all of the other notes on that string out of position. The best use of this is for certain pieces that will take a recurring pedal-point bass. One such number is "The Blues" (Ex. 36, page 58). The low guitar note does much to establish the brooding mood of the piece right from the downbeat. This note is repeated throughout the entire number.

The guitar is a good mixer, too. It is especially effective when used in unison with the vibes, the piano, or the celesta.

The Bass Guitar

We have in the bass guitar an instrument that has become very popular over the past few years, especially in the smaller combos. It is amplified and does the same job as the string bass. However, in a big band I have never felt that it generates the power and excitement that the string bass does. Conversely, in a rock band, I would consider it a necessity.

The bass guitar is four-stringed and is tuned the same as the string bass, sounding an octave below where it is written in the bass clef. Check your player before you write:

EXAMPLE 112   *THE BASS GUITAR*
                (4 STRINGS)

The String Bass

The string bass sounds an octave lower than written:

EXAMPLE 113   *THE STRING BASS*

Its safe range extends about an octave above the open G string. Experts go a bit higher.

In ballads or up tunes that take a two-bass-notes-to-the-bar pattern, keep your bass line in the staff with A or Bb as the top note (above the open G string).

Some basses, mostly in symphonic playing, go down to the C below the low E. For a special effect the E string of the conventional dance bass can be tuned down to the C below ("The Blues," Ex. 36, page 58).

In most jazz writing the bass line is of the "walking bass" variety. The opening bars of "Fallout" (*Peter Gunn*), propelled by Rolly Bundock's bass and Jack Sperling on drums, illustrate this much better than words can. Almost without exception the *Peter Gunn* music is based on this rhythmic pattern:

EXAMPLE 114   *FALLOUT*   Side D. Band 4

A variation of the walking bass rhythm is the shuffle rhythm. The bass continues four-to-the-bar, but the rest of the rhythm section sets up a dotted eighth and sixteenth pattern above:

EXAMPLE 115   *"SHUFFLE RHYTHM" NOTATION*

I have seen some scores in which the bass part was a duplication of the guitar part. In other words, just chord symbols. This is only acceptable behind ad lib choruses. To use chord symbols as your bass part behind written sections is deplorable and downright lazy. The bass line is as much a part of the piece as is the melody line. In fact, the bass line tells us more about the writer's real harmonic ability than anything else he puts down on paper.

However, in recent years; especially in rock and country music, chord sheets have become the norm. Record Producers have become the record "producers." The bass guitarist has become the prima donna in the present scheme of things.

The possibility of the bowed bass (arco) should not be overlooked. In out-of-tempo passages a single bowed bass forms a solid bottom for the saxes, the woodwinds, the brasses, or the strings. Here it is imperative that the bass stay under the open G string—the lower the better.

Since most of our examples include bass parts, a review of this book with an eye on these parts will give you a good idea of the capabilities of the string bass. Notice particularly that the walking bass line rarely settles on the same note for two successive beats. It usually moves, scalewise or chordwise. If a situation comes up where the same bass note is imperative on two successive beats, try jumping the octave either up or down and then move on. Extra time spent in developing your bass line is time well spent.

The Drums

The drummer's basic equipment consists of a snare drum, a bass drum, a foot cymbal (also called the top hat or sock cymbal), two tom-toms (one small and mounted on the bass drum, the other quite a bit larger and sitting on the side opposite the foot cymbal), and two large cymbals (one called the top or ride cymbal and used mostly behind solos; the other, the crash or fast cymbal, used to hit accents along with the band). A pair of drumsticks and a pair of wire brushes round out the drummer's tools. This only takes acoustic drums into account. The sophistication of synthesized drums and drum machines is mind boggling. Close communication with your drummer, or synthesizist, is the only thing I can advise on this subject.

Lest the arranger get writer's cramp notating the drum part, here are the accepted abbreviations for all of his equipment:

Snare drum	Sn.	Large tom-tom	Lr. T.T.
Bass drum	B. D.	Top cymbal	Tp. Cym.
Foot cymbal	F. C.	Ride cymbal	Rd. Cym.
Top hat	T. H.	Crash cymbal	Cr. Cym.
Sock cymbal	S. C.	Sticks	St.
Small tom-tom	Sm. T.T.	Wire brushes	Br.

Most drummers have a set of timpani mallets that they use on the large cymbals or on the large tom-tom in tutti passages. You can also count on a triangle (Tr.) and a woodblock (W.B.) being available. Check with your drummer and you will find that he has an attic full of things out of which he can get some sort of sound.

The drum part is written on a single staff in the bass clef. The four-to-the-bar walking bass pattern is indicated:

EXAMPLE 116

The two-beat pattern is indicated:

EXAMPLE 117

The bottom note is used for the bass drum and the top note is used for anything you wish. If you should want brushes on snare, indicate "Br. on Sn." above the top line.

The foot cymbal is practically automatic on the second and fourth beats no matter what the hands are doing.

Cymbals are indicated:

EXAMPLE 118   *CYMBAL NOTATION*

It is a good idea to indicate at every eight or sixteen bars who has the lead. In pieces that have extended ad lib solos it is permissible to use an abbreviated notation:

EXAMPLE 119

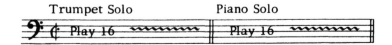

Once more we have a situation where the written part is only a guide. Try out different drum sounds during rehearsal and find the ones that suit your arrangement best. However, you can indicate on the part whether you want brushes, sticks, cymbals, etc., thereby giving the drummer a general idea of what you have in mind.

The Timpani

Although not usually available in the danceband, the timpani are standard equipment in recording work. The four basic drums are tuned:

EXAMPLE 120   *THE (BASIC) TIMPANI*

Modern timpani are tuned by means of a sliding pedal that is operated with the foot. The drums can be tuned very quickly even while the rest of the orchestra is playing. Many types of mallets are available.

One of the principal jobs of the timpani is to bolster the bass line in tutti passages.

An example of a more subtle usage can be found in "Floating Pad" (Ex. 37, page 59). The timpani doubles the string bass very softly while Shelly Manne tastefully performs an exotic rhythm on timbales and tom-toms.

A study of some of the contemporary symphonic works will reveal that the timpanist's role can demand the utmost in skill and taste.

The Vibraphone

Gone are the days when the vibraphone was used exclusively for bell notes and arpeggios. Today's vibe man is an integral part of any group that is fortunate enough to have him.

The vibraphone is a non-transposing instrument:

EXAMPLE 121   *THE VIBRAPHONE*

Sounds as written:

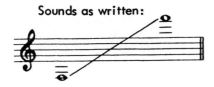

Most of the jazz solo work is done with two mallets but practically all players can handle three or four mallets at the same time. Three- or four-note chords can be played with ease at a slow or moderate tempo. The trouble begins when you have several four-note chords following each other in rapid succession.

The vibraphone has a sustaining pedal and can hold onto a note or chord for just about as long as the pedaled piano can.

There is also a vibrato control on most instruments. The vibrato can be turned off, giving a cold, straight sound preferred by some soloists. Some of the modern jazz school of players use the vibrato, moving at a very low rate of speed. This gives a slow, pronounced, pulsating effect on sustained notes. The very fast vibrato is very uncommon, especially in the jazz field.

There are several different kinds of mallets, ranging from hard to soft. The hard ones produce a slight metallic ping. The softer the mallets, the softer the attack.

Our first example shows the melody being played in octaves. It occurs in the first release of "Lightly" (*More Peter Gunn*):

EXAMPLE 122   *LIGHTLY*   Side E, Band 1

"Joanna" (Ex. 32, page 52) has the vibes starting out playing a triad and then joining the lead alto flute near the end of the phrase.

In the intro of "Timothy" (Ex. 22, page 38), the vibes double the trombones on the opening rhythmic pattern. The metallic sound adds an unusual color to the muted trombones.

An overworked effect that is typical of the vibraphone is the shimmer or smear. In this, the player puts his sustaining pedal down and proceeds to play a chromatic scale lightly up and down for several octaves, ad lib. The notes all run together, creating an ethereal effect.

This is written:

EXAMPLE 123   *NOTATION OF "SHIMMER" (OR "SMEAR")*

The vibraphone is called upon many times to feed soloists. In these cases simply write out the guitar chord symbols and write "B. G." (background) at the beginning of that particular passage.

This is an extremely colorful instrument. Its wooden bars create a unique sound that has many orchestral uses. The marimba range:

EXAMPLE 124   *THE MARIMBA*

The top octave has a sound very much like that of the xylophone. When played with hard mallets it is a good substitute for the xylophone. Unlike the vibraphone, the marimba has no sustaining pedal. Once a note is struck it soon vanishes. The only way to sustain a note or chord is by the use of tremolo.

In "Night Flower" (*Mr. Lucky*) the marimba playing tremolo doubles the unison strings and horns at the beginning of the second chorus:

EXAMPLE 125   *NIGHT FLOWER*   Side E, Band 1

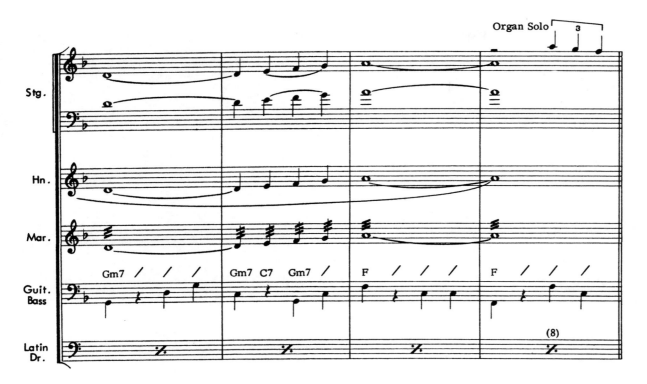

The four-mallet chordal tremolo is used in "My Friend Andamo" (*Mr. Lucky*) behind the unison strings in the first release:

EXAMPLE 126   *MY FRIEND ANDAMO*   Side E, Band 1

"One-Eyed Cat" (Ex. 41, page 63) has our man playing a triad on the after-beats, always a good effect for this type of piece.

"Tipsy" (Ex. 27, page 46) shows the marimba doubling the piano.

The first statement of the theme in "March of the Cue Balls" (*Mr. Lucky*) is an example of the rhythm ensemble carrying the lead. The marimba is joined by the guitar, piano, and bass:

EXAMPLE 127   *MARCH OF THE CUE BALLS*   Side E, Band 1

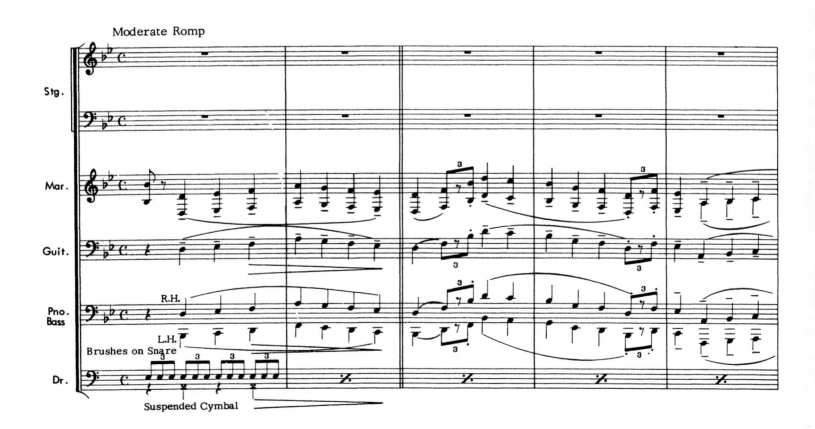

The marimba is a "special" color instrument. It can lend much when used to double other members of the orchestra.

The Xylophone

This is a piccolo of the percussion. The xylophone sound is a striking color when used either for solo or doubling other instruments. It sounds an octave higher than written:

EXAMPLE 128   *THE XYLOPHONE*

The last five bars of "That's It and That's All" (*Mr. Lucky*) show off
its solo talents:

EXAMPLE 129 *THAT'S IT AND THAT'S ALL* Side E, Band 1

In "Chime Time" (Ex. 58, page 88) the xylophone doubles the top piccolo, adding a percussive sound to the woodwinds.

Again in "Lightly Latin" (Ex. 50, page 72) the xylophone gives the woodwind figure a biting sound.

All types of staccato figures are enhanced by the addition of the xylophone. It can play extremely fast passages with ease. Biting brass figures can be colored a bit by adding the xylophone doubling the lead trumpet. One word of caution: The xylophone sound is so piercing and dominating that the ear easily becomes annoyed with it. Pick your spots with care. Its entrance should contain a certain element of surprise to be effective.

The Bells

Also known as the bell-lyre or the glockenspiel, the bells are a welcome addition to our collection of percussion colors. Their delightful, tinkling sound is equally at home with woodwinds, strings, brass, and other mallet percussion.

The bells sound an octave above where they are written:

EXAMPLE 130   *THE BELLS*

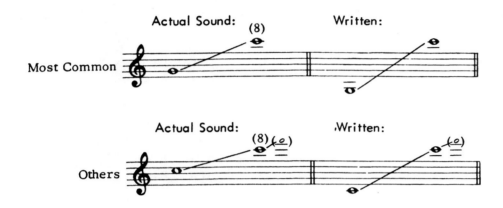

The "Mr. Lucky Theme" (Ex. 26, page 45) is typical of the bells' doubling of the woodwinds.

"Night Flower" (Ex. 52, page 79) again has the bells and the woodwinds together.

The bells have good natural sustaining power. They ring for a while after they are struck unless stopped with the finger.

A good effect that the bells do well is the glissando. The last full bar of "That's It and That's All" (Ex. 129, page 175) is a very clear example of this.

The bells are a charming addition to the melody line of divided strings. They can be used to good advantage with muted brass, whether in biting figures or melodic passages. The bells have almost unlimited uses with members of their own percussion family. Unisons with vibes, xylophone, guitar, celesta, and piano are all useful.

The bell sound is a distinctive one. Use it wisely and sparingly.

The Harp

The modern harp is tuned to the diatonic scale of C♭ major:

EXAMPLE 131   *THE HARP*

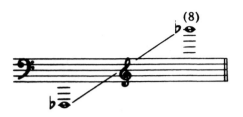

The harp has seven pedals, one for each note in the diatonic scale. With all seven pedals in the flat position, the Cb major scale results. With all of the pedals depressed into the second notch (natural) the Cb scale becomes a C♮ diatonic scale. Depressed to the lowest notch (sharp) the C♮ scale becomes a C# diatonic scale. You can readily see that chromatic scales and consecutive chromatic arpeggios and broken chords are impossible. Consecutive arpeggios and broken chords, having no common notes, are impractical. The harpist can manipulate almost anything else.

The notation of the harp part in today's commercial field has been simplified from the more complete notation in legitimate writing. The professional harpist is thoroughly familiar with the chord symbol system.

The glissando, the ever-present bane of the harpist's existence, can be notated in several ways. Since the harp cannot gliss on a four-note chord the player will add the ninth to the dominant seventh chord whether it is indicated or not. The same is true of the major sixth chord.

The following are based on the G seventh chord:

EXAMPLE 132

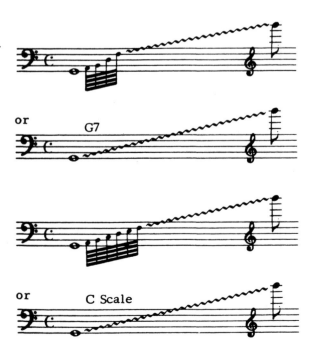

The G sixth chord. Shown here while the orchestra is sustaining a final tutti chord:

EXAMPLE 133

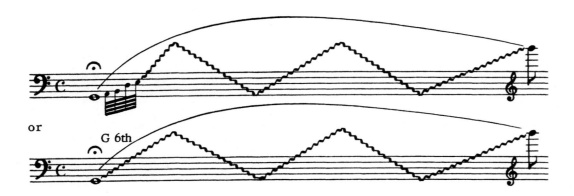

The harpist will gliss ad lib until the conductor gives the cut-off.

The glissando needn't start low. It can be reversed to start high and go downward. It can also be played in thirds or sixths. For all forms of altered chord glissandi, either write out the first octave of notes you wish or simply write down the chord symbols. The player will figure out his own method of execution.

Broken chords and arpeggios are written out exactly as you wish them played. Chord symbols are not used here. Keep in mind that the harpist can only play four notes in each hand since the little finger is not used.

Unfortunately the harpist in the commercial field is called upon to use only a minute part of his full capabilities as a player. If you decide to get a little fancy with your harp part, have no fear that it will not be played.

Latin Instruments
and Rhythms

CHAPTER SEVEN

Latin Instruments and Rhythms

A PARTIAL LIST OF THE BASIC INSTRUMENTS:

Timbales   (with cowbell)
Conga Drum
Bongos
Claves
Maracas
Guiro   (gourd)
Jaw Bone
Cabaza   (beaded gourd)
Boo-Bams   (a relatively new entry in the Latin field. Authentic boo-bams are made from hollowed-out bamboo stalks. There can be any number of them to a set, up to twelve. Although definite pitch is not necessary they sometimes come tuned accurately to a diatonic or chromatic scale. The sound is similar to that of the bongos but is lighter and more transparent.)

All Latin rhythms do not include all of the Latin instruments. Two or three drummers can take care of just about any of the various rhythms. However, the following examples show the full percussion section in action:

EXAMPLE 134   *CHA-CHA RHYTHM—A MODERATE 4*

EXAMPLE 135   *MAMBO RHYTHM—A BRIGHT 4*

EXAMPLE 136   *SAMBA RHYTHM—A MODERATE
TO BRIGHT 2*

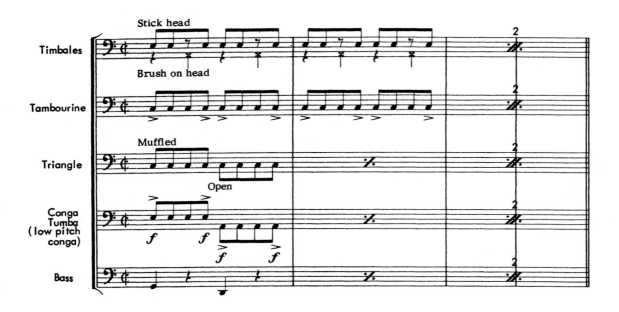

EXAMPLE 137   *RHUMBA RHYTHM—A SLOW TO
MODERATE 4*

EXAMPLE 138   *AFRO-BOLERO RHYTHM—A SLOW BALLAD IN 4*

EXAMPLE 139   *MERINGUE RHYTHM—A VERY BRIGHT 2*

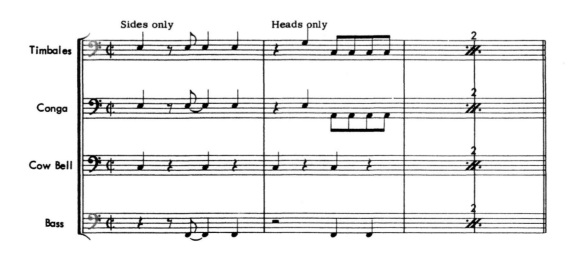

EXAMPLE 140   *BAION RHYTHM—A SLOW TO
MODERATE 4*

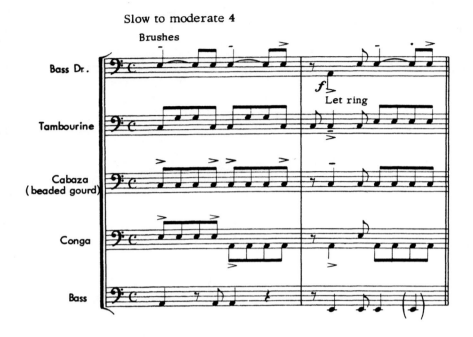

EXAMPLE 141   *BOSSA NOVA*

* Sealed can containing rice or sand.

To pin down the piano and guitar parts is an almost impossible task, owing to the ad lib nature of the rhythms. The best you can do is to give the chord symbols (and the bass part for the piano) and let them work themselves into the rest of the rhythm section. However, the written guitar pattern in *Bossa Nova* is an integral part of the rhythm.

With experienced professionals all that is really needed on the drum parts is an indication of what type of rhythm is wanted. They will do the rest.*

---

* My sincere thanks to Milt Holland for his expert assistance in this chapter.

The Combo

CHAPTER EIGHT

The Combo

HOW TO WRITE FOR A SMALL GROUP HAS ALWAYS BEEN A knotty problem for the novice. The combo with its limited instrumentation is a real challenge to the arranger. He must approach this task with the idea of making his combo sound as good as possible, not as big as possible.

After the piano intro, "Not from Dixie" (*Peter Gunn*) presents an octave unison: trumpet and alto sax on the top line; trombone and baritone sax on the lower. The trumpet and alto sax in unison is one of the more basic small-group sounds. This particular passage could have been written without the lower octave doubling. The release has the instruments in a four-way, closely-voiced position:

EXAMPLE 142   *NOT FROM DIXIE*   Side E, Band 2

The piano and the guitar set up a drone fifth pattern at the start of "Sorta Blue" (*Peter Gunn*). The alto sax, the baritone sax, the trombone, and the vibes then enter with the unison theme. The release has two forms of open voicing. The first four bars, a medium spread, the second four very wide:

EXAMPLE 143   *SORTA BLUE*   Side E, Band 2

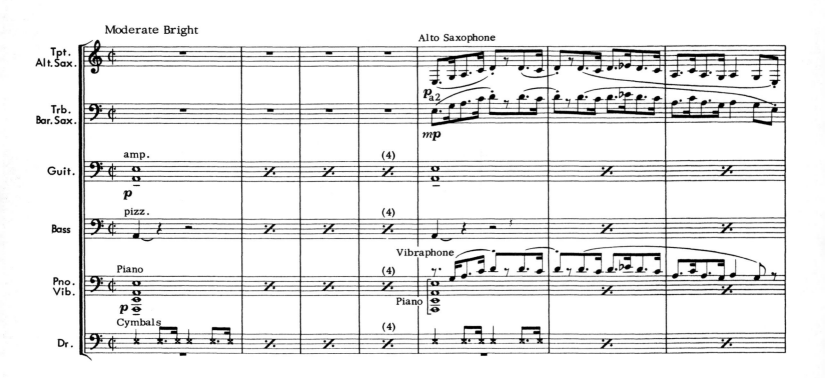

In numbers where several ad lib solos follow each other it is a good idea to break up the solos a bit by having your ensemble "kick off" into one of the solos. This is an old device in jazz, but it never fails to give a lift. Our example occurs a bit further down in "Sorta Blue" (*Peter Gunn*):

EXAMPLE 144　　*SORTA BLUE*　　　　　　　　　　　　　　Side E, Band 2

"Goofin' at the Coffee House" (*More Peter Gunn*) has a four-way unison in the first strain: cup-muted trumpet, alto flute, alto sax, and vibes:

EXAMPLE 145   *GOOFIN' AT THE COFFEE HOUSE*   Side E, Band 3

Getting into a smaller group we have the alto flute and cup-muted trombone starting off "The Brothers Go to Mother's" (*Peter Gunn*):

EXAMPLE 146   *THE BROTHERS GO TO MOTHER'S*   Side E, Band 3

On the last eight of the first chorus, a repeat of the opening theme, the trombone opens up and the alto flute changes to alto sax, making for quite a contrast to the opening statement.

The first chorus of "A Profound Gass" (*Peter Gunn*) presents the alto flute, the guitar, and the vibes in unison. Notice that the piano is written out at the ninth bar. The correct voicing of the piano chords here was necessary to the composition. Chord symbols would have been a hit or miss proposition:

EXAMPLE 147 *A PROFOUND GASS* Side E, Band 3

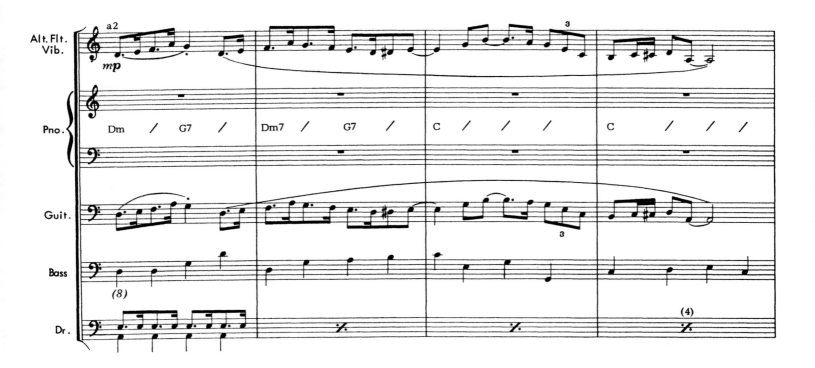

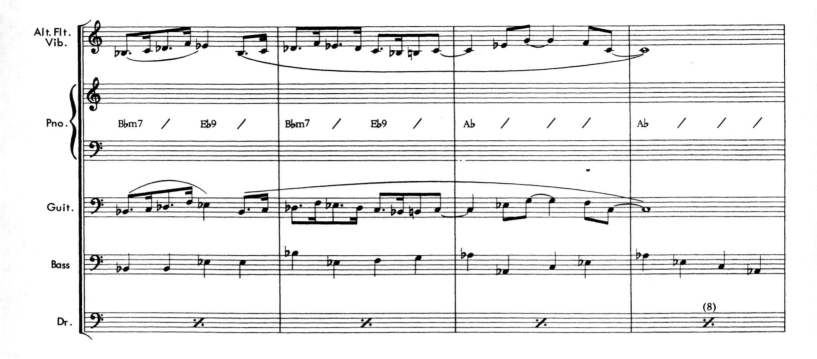

"Lightly" (*More Peter Gunn*) takes us into a still smaller group. The opening eight bars are a tutti unison. The second eight have the guitar and the piano forming a walking bass pattern in tenths against the vibes and guitar lead:

EXAMPLE 148   *LIGHTLY*   Side F, Band 1

A bit later in the same number, after the guitar solo, we have an ensemble with the guitar and the vibes playing the lead in octaves and the piano filling in the harmony with five-way block chords. This is the famous George Shearing sound:

EXAMPLE 149   *LIGHTLY*

This particular sound is very useful for slow ballads such as "A Quiet Gass" (*More Peter Gunn*).

EXAMPLE 150   *A QUIET GASS*

Side F, Band 1

All of the preceding examples serve to show only a few of the possibilities of the jazz oriented combo.

The String Section

CHAPTER NINE

The String Section

COMMERCIAL WRITING DEMANDS A WORKING KNOWLEDGE OF the string section. The arranger must be able to handle a string group of any size.

The violin, the viola, and the cello are extremely versatile instruments. Dynamically, they go instantly from a double *pianissimo* to a double *forte*. Dramatically, their range is practically endless. The light, airy passages or the broad, somber ones are played with equal ease. Technically, just about anything is possible. The string family, of course, is a non-transposing group. With the exception of the string bass they sound where they are written. The open strings are tuned:

EXAMPLE 151   *VIOLIN, VIOLA, CELLO*

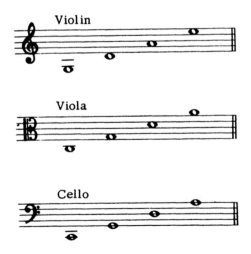

The viola is written in the alto clef (). Middle C is on the third line. Its open strings are C, G, D, and A.

Double, triple, and quadruple stops are possible on all three instruments. These stops are indicated by a bracket:

EXAMPLE 152

This means that two, three, or four notes are fingered and played at the same time. The simple and obvious rule to follow in figuring out if a particular stop is possible is this: make sure that you don't have two notes on the same string. In the case of three- or four-note stops at least one of the notes should be on an open string, and with a four-note chord it is preferable to have two open strings. The open strings give resonance to the chord.

Double stops can be sustained practically as well as single notes. However, triple and quadruple notes cannot be sustained because the bow cannot touch all of the notes at the same time. These chords are usually bowed or plucked very quickly from the bottom up.

The final chord in "That's It and That's All" (Ex. 129, page 175) illustrates this.

The proper notation for the various types of bowing can save much time and conversation at rehearsals. However, unless you are a string player and can mark the bowings exactly as you want them you should take the advice and suggestions of your first violinist (concertmaster). In the case of the *Mr. Lucky* orchestra, he is the most capable Erno Neufeld.

> Arco means bowed.
> Pizzicato (pizz.) means plucked.
> The up-bow is marked: V
> The down-bow is marked: ⊓

Legato

EXAMPLE 153

Notice that there are no slur marks above the notes. The player will automatically give one separate bow to each note, alternating up and down. This can become quite emotional, depending on how much of the bow the player uses. The longer the bow strokes, the more dramatic and forceful the feeling.

Another legato bowing:

EXAMPLE 154

Here he plays the first four notes in one down-bow and the next four up-bow, ending with the last note on a down-bow. This is usually a more placid and tranquil sound than our first legato example. Combinations of these two types of legato are common. Unless indicated otherwise the down-beat of a phrase will take a down-bow and a pickup upbeat an up-bow.

Détaché

Here we have a type of bowing that is neither legato nor staccato but a combination of both:

EXAMPLE 155

The bow does not leave the string. This is an extremely dramatic effect regardless of tempo.

Louré

This is a derivative of détaché. The difference is that several notes are played in one bow with a very slight separation between the notes, usually very softly. The slurs indicate the bow changes:

EXAMPLE 156

Staccato

Very short alternate up and down bows create the staccato effect.

EXAMPLE 157

Spiccato

This is notated the same as staccato, the difference being that the bow has more of a bouncing-on-the-string feeling. Spiccato or saltando should be written on the part if you want this effect.

Jeté

This is another bouncing-bow device. The bow is permitted to bounce on the string, playing a group of notes until the player changes the direction of the bow. The slur indicates the notes that are to be played in one bow:

EXAMPLE 158

Consecutive down-bows will give a stark, heavy, accented sound. The bow is lifted off the string for each note:

EXAMPLE 159

Sur la touche (sul tasto)

The bow engages the strings over the fingerboard further away from the bridge than normal. The sound is very soft and transparent.

Ponticello

A thin and chilling sound is created by bowing very close to the bridge. This is used mostly with tremolo.

Col legno

The bow is turned over and the wooden shaft strikes the strings. This is best used for staccato passages.

To cancel out the above-mentioned effects, mark "Normal" or "Natural" on the parts.

Portamento

This is a means of connecting two consecutive notes, usually a skip of a third or more, by sliding from one to the other. It is used in broad, melodic passages. Portamento is indicated by a straight line between two notes:

EXAMPLE 160

Vibrato

By pulsating the finger over a held note the vibrato is created. The degree of vibrato is easily controlled. An extremely icy sound can be achieved by omission of the vibrato altogether. This is marked "N.V." (no vibrato).

Sul G
Sul D
Sul A
Sul E

When the part is marked with any of the above, the passage is played solely on that string. Sul G is most frequently used:

EXAMPLE 161

Expressive (Expr.) lets the player know that a little extra feeling is wanted.

Tremolo

There are two kinds of tremolo: bowed and fingered. The bowed tremolo is indicated:

EXAMPLE 162

Each of the notes can be attacked for another effect:

EXAMPLE 163

The bowed tremolo has a full dynamic range, from *pianissimo* to *fortissimo*.

The fingered tremolo can be produced starting with the interval of a minor third. Anything under that interval is called a trill. For best results in both the trill and fingered tremolo, try to avoid putting one of the notes on an open string. The player has little to "hold onto" when an open string is involved. The fingered tremolo is notated:

EXAMPLE 164

The trill:

EXAMPLE 165

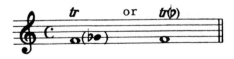

"Let's Walk" (*Mancini Touch*) has the full string section performing the fingered tremolo:

EXAMPLE 166   *LET'S WALK*   Side F, Band 2

Harmonics

The harmonics are divided into two groups, the natural and the artificial. The natural group are all derived from the open strings. The artificial harmonics are stopped with the fingers. The open string (natural harmonics):

EXAMPLE 167

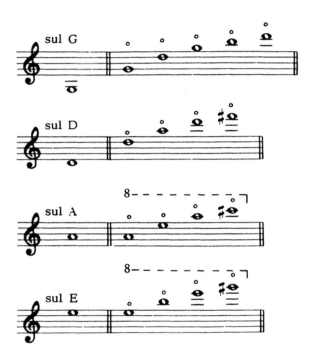

The artificial harmonics are notated:

EXAMPLE 168

As you can readily see, many of the harmonics can be played in several ways. Don't worry about this. Let the player choose his own method of execution.

Both the viola and the cello have the same harmonic structure as the violin.

String mutes

The use of mutes (sordini) produces a haunting and somewhat hollow sound. Simply mark the parts "mutes" (or sordini) when you wish them on; "mutes off" (or senza sordini) when you wish them off. Allow a bit of time to put them on and take them off. If you can't spare the strings the necessary time off to place or remove the mutes, you may do this: about eight bars before the muted passage, write "mutes on one by one." By the time your muted passage comes up all of the players will have put the mutes on without an obvious interruption of the string line. They can be removed in the same manner.

Two string players read from each stand. In larger sections where many duplications of the same part are necessary, the copyist makes a master copy on onion skin paper and then runs off as many parts as are needed on a duplicating machine.

On the actual score paper, one or two staves for the violins and one staff each for the violas and cellos are usually adequate for the smaller sections. For the large sections, three staves for the violins and two each for the violas and cellos can be used.

Be extremely careful with your syncopated phrasings. Jazz notation has yet to be proved practical for the string section.

The "Mr. Lucky Theme" (*Mr. Lucky*) leads us into our first example of divisi string writing. Our section is twelve violins, four violas, and four cellos. Always indicate how many players should be on each part. In this case, six on the lead and two each on the other three parts in the violins. Since there are four violas and four cellos, no marking is needed, because it is obvious that there are two on a part.

With fewer violins you would cut down on the number playing the lead. Ten violins would be divided: 4-2-2-2. Eight violins: 2-2-2-2. In this type of voicing ("Mr. Lucky Theme") four violas and four cellos are the minimum you can use and expect a good, full sound.

(NOTE: When the violas and cellos are written high the treble clef is used. The tenor clef is also used where applicable.)

EXAMPLE 169   *MR. LUCKY*   Side F, Band 2

The second eight bars of the same number have the strings getting down behind the four French horns lead (Ex. 73, page 107).

In this section the violas and cellos go from two divisi notes to a single note, depending on the chord structure. This does not effect the over-all balance of the section. Strings have a great faculty of balancing within themselves.

In "Lightly" (Ex. 55, page 82), we have the close five-way voicing with the cellos doubling the violin lead an octave lower. Since the lead is doubled in the lower octave by the cellos, we distribute our violins 4-4-4, thus giving a stronger over-all sound to the passage.

In "Chime Time" (*Mr. Lucky*) the strings, following the organ solo, provide a good illustration of both the close voicing (first two bars) and then the open voicing:

EXAMPLE 170   *CHIME TIME*   Side F, Band 3

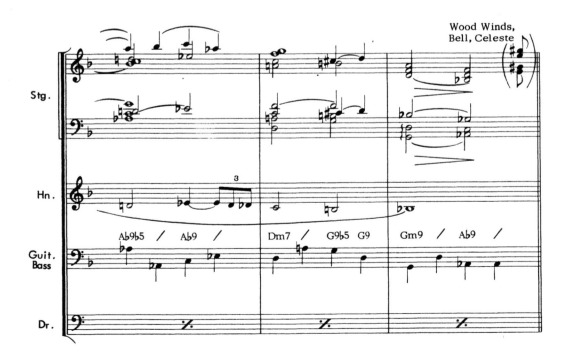

The broad low-register string unison is probably the most dramatic and moving sound in the orchestra. No matter what the size of the section the low unison is always effective.

In "Night Flower" (*Mr. Lucky*), after the valve trombone has played the first sixteen bars, the violas and cellos are joined by the four horns in an extremely sonorous passage. With the return of the trombone the strings divide to form the background:

EXAMPLE 171 *NIGHT FLOWER* Side F, Band 3

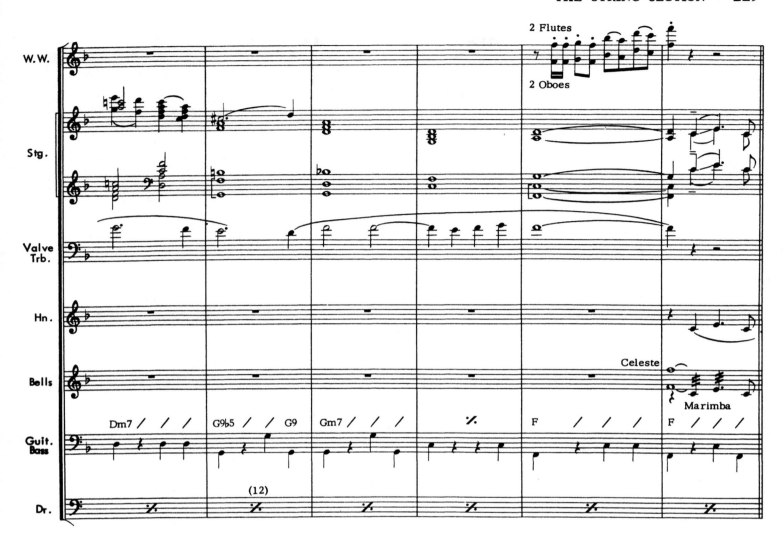

Directly following the previous example we have the violins, the violas, the cellos, and the horns picking up the melody in a full-bodied unison ("Night Flower," Ex. 125, page 170).

"My Friend Andamo" (Ex. 126, page 171) is a good illustration of the pure unison string sound.

The violas and the cellos playing divisi provide a well-sounding background. It is a good change in color from the "violins on top" voicing ("A Cool Shade of Blue," Ex. 34, page 55).

The violas and cellos can also be written in close position. Certain melodies lend themselves to this treatment:

EXAMPLE 172

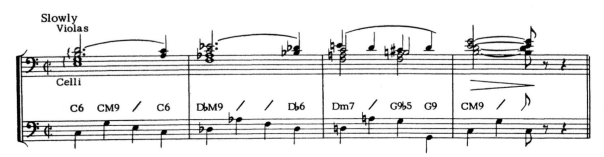

"Blue Satin" (*Mr. Lucky*) provides a good illustration of ensemble writing involving the strings with the rest of the orchestra. The strings take over the melody (aided by three piccolos) in the last eight bars of the second chorus. The four trombones form the harmonic background and the horns sing out the counter-melody. Although not on the record, three trumpets have been cued in to show their role under these conditions:

EXAMPLE 173   *BLUE SATIN*   Side F, Band 4

A similar situation is recalled in "Softly" (Ex. 24, page 44).

The second release of "Floating Pad" (*Mr. Lucky*) is another illustration of the full-bodied tutti:

EXAMPLE 174   *FLOATING PAD*   Side F, Band 4

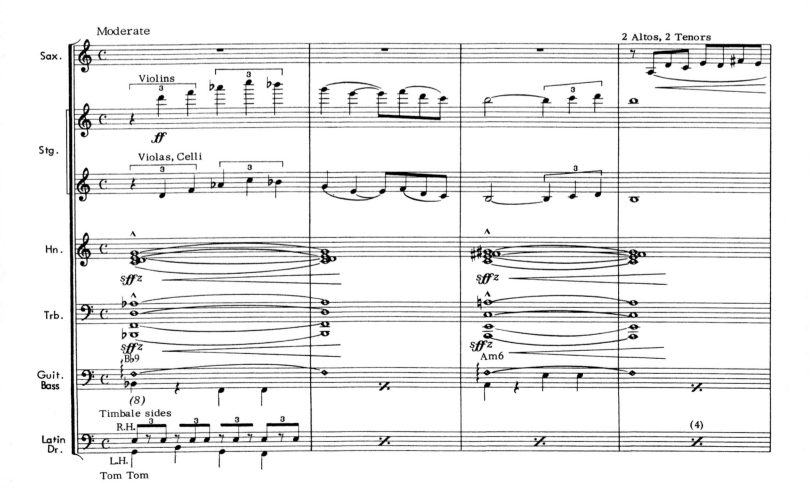

Next is a full orchestra consisting of six brass, five woodwinds (two flutes, two clarinets, and a baritone sax), four horns, twenty strings (twelve violins, four violas, four cellos), and rhythm. This is scored in a definitely grandiose style with an over-used but definitely usable "Paramount" ending.

The baritone sax is used to reinforce the brass. Any additional low woodwinds, such as bass clarinet or bassoon, would be given the bottom part. Any additional high woodwinds would double the present woodwind line:

Example 175   *JOANNA*

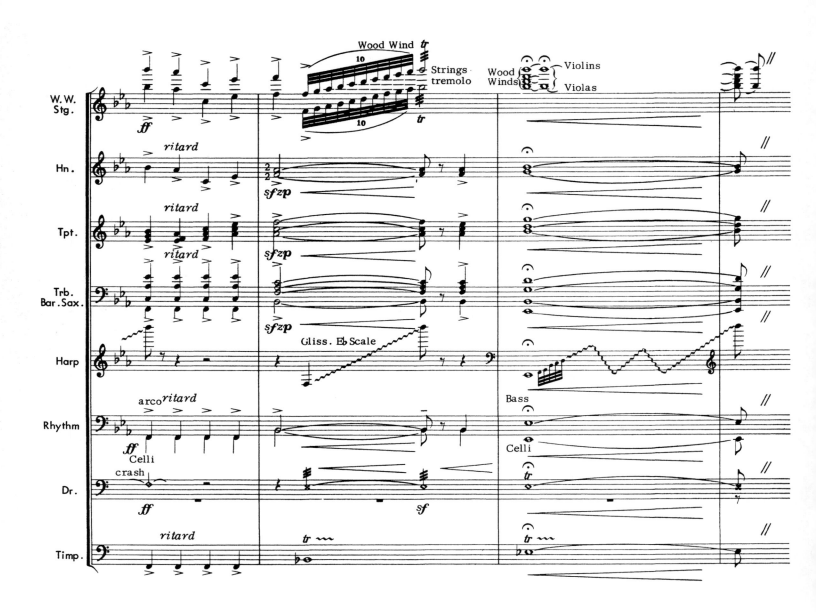

The strings have a gay side too. They can be light and lilting on occasion. "March of the Cue Balls" (Ex. 49, page 67) contains such a passage. The strings and the woodwinds romp along over the trombones pumping out the melody.

Later in the same number the violins and the violas, doubling the piccolos and the oboes, respectively, provide a whirlwind background to the horns' and the trombones' lead. The cellos go below to help out the string bass:

EXAMPLE 176   *MARCH OF THE CUE BALLS*   Side F, Band 5

The doubling of the cellos and the bass is common both in arco and pizzicato passages. A typical pizzicato passage can be found in "One-Eyed Cat" (Ex. 41, page 63). One word of caution about this type of doubling: Never do it in a walking bass passage. The legitimate cellist is not known for his ability to swing.

Low legato passages with the cellos and the bass playing in octaves create a dramatic and moody sound. In out-of-tempo passages when the strings play divisi, the arco bass has two possibilities: double the bottom cello line in unison or an octave below; or play the bass note alone (necessary when the bass note is below the cello range). Both ways are shown:

EXAMPLE 177

The last six bars of "One-Eyed Cat" (*Mr. Lucky*) gets us back into a lighter mood:

EXAMPLE 178   *ONE-EYED CAT*   Side F, Band 5

Let's take a return visit to "Chime Time" (Ex. 23, page 42). Pizzicato is put to good use here.

Our previous examples have utilized a fairly large string section. For commercial recording this is an ideal size, although the average recording section used for vocal backgrounds is more often eight violins, two violas, two cellos.

Modern recording techniques are extremely flattering to the strings. A well-recorded string section will sound much larger than it actually is.

The treatment of a smaller section in non-recorded writing is another matter. A different approach must be taken because a violin divisi conceived for twelve or fourteen cannot be made to sound as good for four or six. Unisons for a few violins sound good in the lower and medium registers, but they get progressively thinner as they get up into the high range.

A good pattern to follow in your string writing for a small section is that of a string quartet. This is as ideal for a section consisting of four violins, one viola, and one cello as it is for the largest of string groups:

EXAMPLE 179

The double-stop fifth in the cello is a frequently used means of getting another voice into the chord, especially when the fifth of the chord gets below the viola range. If our group is six violins, one viola, and one cello, the same voicing would be used except that we would divide the violins four and two. However, six violins permits us to add a fifth voice and another approach to our previous example:

EXAMPLE 180

Thirds and doubled thirds in octaves are a good device for a small section. The woodwinds lend support in the lower harmonies, as both types of thirds are shown:

EXAMPLE 181

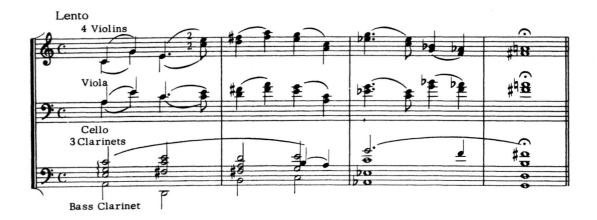

The tutti string unison is very useful in a small section. The best range for this is from the low violin G up to the B♭ a minor tenth above. This keeps the viola and cello in a sensible and sonorous range.

The string section in most dance orchestras is always the hopelessly outnumbered minority. Conceive the string parts with this in mind; the soaring string sounds of the larger orchestra are simply not possible with a small section.

CHAPTER TEN

Conclusion

THERE WAS A TIME WHEN THE LINES SEPARATING POP, Jazz, Rock, Folk, Country, Latin, and Rhythm and Blues were clearly defined. These lines are being crossed with increased frequency as new and influential performers and writers continue to emerge. A change in basic concept often follows innovation. We are now involved in such a change of concept that has influenced the entire orchestra—live synthesized sound. The electric organ and guitar were the forerunners, of course. The piano and even the harpsichord have been wired for sound. The entire saxophone and woodwind families are now involved. The string family is a prime candidate. Even the solo brasses. New and useful synthesizers have emerged. To ignore this movement in the electronics field would be a serious mistake. Our job deals with musical sound, regardless of its source.

The milk of sacred cows has a way of turning sour. The entire music scene is constantly changing, leaving the narrow-minded and the lazy behind. That which is far out today becomes commonplace tomorrow. The truly professional writer must keep up with the ever shifting scene. The man who writes for hire has an obligation, if only to himself, to keep an open mind and to absorb new ideas.